A QUITE INTERESTING BOOK

1,342 QI FACTS

TO LEAVE YOU FLABBERGASTED

Compiled by
John Lloyd, John Mitchinson,
James Harkin & Anne Miller

with the QI Elves
Alex Bell, Mandy Fenton, Andrew Hunter Murray,
Anna Ptaszynski & Dan Schreiber

First published in 2016
by Faber & Faber Ltd
Bloomsbury House
74–77 Great Russell Street
London WC1B 3DA
This paperback edition first published in 2017

Typeset by Ian Bahrami
Printed and bound in England by CPI Group (UK) Ltd,
Croydon CR0 4YY

A CIP record for this book
is available from the British Library

ISBN 978–0–571–33247–2

2 4 6 8 10 9 7 5 3

Contents

[v]

Read This First

This may *look* like a book, but it's actually a *portal*.

While you can read the whole thing in a couple of hours, each little nugget is just the visible tip of an information iceberg.

So, if you doubt any of the facts, or would like to know more, go online to:

qi.com/1342

In the search box, enter the *page number* of the fact that interests you. Here you'll find our main source for each fact laid out in a mirror image, as shown overleaf.

| Page in book | Page in source finder |

Click on the link (or check out the print source) to get the full explanation and all the background details.

To our surprise, we've found this feature is of particular value to teachers, who can start each lesson with a QI fact related to what they have to say.

When asked 'Why?', the teacher (having read the source material) can confidently say: 'I'll tell you exactly why . . .'

But you don't need to be a teacher to do this – you can educate yourself.

It's what the four of us have been doing every working day these last few years.

We hope you'll be as flabbergasted as we were.

JOHN LLOYD, JOHN MITCHINSON,
JAMES HARKIN & ANNE MILLER

*The truth is
more important
than the facts.*
FRANK LLOYD WRIGHT
(1867–1959)

The most distant
object in the universe is
13.42 billion light years away.

To get to the nearest star
at a tenth of the speed of light
would take 42 years and need
fuel weighing as much
as the Sun.

The Sun gets
4 million tons lighter
every second.

Ten-trillionths of
your suntan comes
from stars in galaxies
beyond the Milky Way.

For a billion years,
the only life on Earth was a kind of slime.
Scientists call this period
'the boring billion'.

Scientists alive today
outnumber all the scientists
who ever lived
up to 1980.

Scientists
watching paint dry
in Surrey and Lyon in 2016
said the results were
'exciting'.

To avoid exciting men,
early bicycles for women
had a 'cherry screen' to
hide their ankles.

No one knows
why bicycles
stay upright.

No one knows
how much money
is in circulation.

Economists
can't explain
boom or bust.

No one knows
why scientists don't
have tails.

The first scientifically named
dinosaur bone was called *Scrotum humanum*
because it looked like a giant pair
of human testicles.

The remains of
a dinosaur named
Aachenosaurus multidens
turned out to be lumps
of petrified wood.

Velociraptors
were no bigger
than turkeys.

Dinosaurs didn't roar;
they mumbled
or cooed.

Sabre-toothed tigers
never existed.

Neanderthals are
shown as slouching because
the first one to be reconstructed
happened to have arthritis.

The first Neanderthal skull
discovered was thought to belong
to a Cossack with rickets,
the pain of which had
furrowed his brow.

In 2015, Spanish workers
destroyed a 6,000-year-old Neolithic tomb,
mistaking it for a broken picnic table.
They replaced it with a 'better'
picnic table.

When spun on a table,
a US 'Lincoln Memorial' one-cent coin
will land on tails
80% of the time.

The surface area of a cat,
including each hair of its fur,
is 100 times that of its skin
and is enough to cover a
ping-pong table.

Ping-pong balls
have been made larger to
make the sport better
for television.

After *EastEnders*,
so many kettles are turned on
that Britain has to borrow
power from France.

In France,
Germany, Austria, Spain and
the Netherlands they serve
beer in McDonald's.

McNuggets come
in four official shapes:
bell, bone, boot
and ball.

Slit-faced bats are the
only mammals in the world
with a T-shaped tail.

Batman flies
through the air so fast
that landing would
probably kill him.

A 'batman' was a unit of weight
in the Ottoman Empire.
Ben Affleck weighs
about nine
batmans.

In the *X-Men* movies,
the sound of Wolverine's claws
shooting out was made by
tearing a turkey apart.

In the *Halloween* movies,
the killer wears a
Captain Kirk mask,
sprayed white.

In *The Empire Strikes Back*,
the emperor had a man's voice,
a woman's face and a
chimpanzee's eyes.

In *Raiders of the Lost Ark*,
the sound of the boulder that
chased Indiana Jones was made
by rolling a car down
a gravel road.

If every car in Monaco
took to the roads at the same time,
they wouldn't all fit on.

In 2009, the mayors
of adjoining Parisian suburbs
declared the same street as one-way,
but in different directions.

The bridge known as
the 'Gateway to Bolton' is
a one-way street leading
away from Bolton.

In 1845, a bridge
collapsed in Great Yarmouth,
killing 79 people watching
a clown in a tub being
pulled by geese.

Mice
sing like birds,
but humans can't
hear them.

The Elizabethans treated warts
by cutting a mouse in half
and applying it to the
affected part.

Georgian women
worried about mice
getting into their
wigs at night.

The hair of
Twiggy's waxwork
at Madame Tussauds was
dressed by Twiggy's
hairdresser.

A hairdresser in Madrid
cuts hair using a samurai sword
and a blowtorch.

In 1942,
an Italian hairdresser called
'the Phantom Barber of Pascagoula'
broke into people's houses
and cut their hair.

The people most likely
to suffer injuries at work
are hairdressers.

The Smithsonian Museum
has a framed collection of
locks of hair from the
first 14 presidents.

Benjamin Franklin
had a pulley system so he
could lock his bedroom door
from his bed.

Thomas Jefferson
kept a flock of geese
to supply quills
for his pens.

Ronald Reagan
was a stand-up comedian
for two weeks.

The US Senate has
never formally endorsed
the title 'President'.

Franklin D. Roosevelt
and Theodore Roosevelt
pronounced their surnames
differently.

Benjamin Franklin and John Adams
once shared a room and couldn't agree
whether to open or shut the window.
Franklin won by arguing
until Adams fell asleep.

Paper towels
in the White House
are embossed with the
Presidential Seal.

Wasps
were making paper
long before humans existed.

80% of the
€500 notes in Spain are
used for criminal
purposes.

To carry
$10 million in notes
you'd need a minimum of
seven and a half
briefcases.

For a few months
in 1993, Moldova's
official currency was
the *cupon*.

The word 'Czech'
is Polish.

The Czech phrase
strč prst skrz krk, meaning
'thrust finger through neck',
contains no vowels.

There are more than
100 words in Hawaiian
consisting entirely
of vowels.

In ancient Hawaii,
the nuts of the *kukui* tree
were threaded on a string and lit.
Each nut burned in sequence
to form an early version
of chaser lighting.

Ancient Romans
threw walnuts at
the bride.

It takes
five litres of water
to grow a single
almond.

Britain's share
of the cost of funding the
Large Hadron Collider each year
is the same amount of money
as Britons spend
on peanuts.

The cost of the extra fuel needed
to carry a bag of peanuts
on a plane for a year
is £1.

In 2015,
a Singapore Airlines freight plane
made an emergency landing after
farting sheep triggered
the smoke alarm.

Harper Lee,
author of *To Kill a Mockingbird*,
was an airline booking agent.

Woody Allen
writes his film scripts
on a typewriter he bought
in the 1950s.

On a QWERTY keyboard
a typist's fingers cover 20 miles a day;
on a Dvorak keyboard
it's only one mile.

Making all the chain mail
for *The Lord of the Rings* wore
the costume designers'
fingerprints away.

The chants
of the orc army in
The Lord of the Rings were
made by a stadium full
of New Zealand
cricket fans.

The house where
Bilbo Baggins lived
in *The Lord of the Rings* is
now occupied by sheep.

Alexander Graham Bell
tried to breed sheep
with extra nipples.

The longest
human nipple hair was
17 centimetres long.

Gene Roddenberry,
the creator of *Star Trek*,
thought chest hair would
cease to exist in the future.

Hippocrates
used a mixture of
pigeon droppings, horseradish, cumin
and beetroot to treat his hair loss,
but it only made the rest
of his hair fall out.

The Maori
for 'scissors' is
kutikuti.

In Tanzania,
a roundabout is a
kipilefti.

The 'van man'
was around before
the invention of the van:
he used to drive
wagons.

Invented in 1862,
the anti-garrotting cravat
shot spikes into the hands
of anyone attempting to
strangle the wearer.

The inventors
of Silly String were
trying to make a spray-on cast
for broken bones.

Every day,
skateboarding accidents
land 176 American children
in A&E.

At one A&E
in Papua New Guinea,
1 in 40 patients have been hurt
by a falling coconut.

The last person to be
killed by a single hailstone
was a pizza delivery man
in Fort Worth, Texas.

To avoid being hit
by space junk in 2014
the International Space Station (ISS)
had to change orbit three times.

The wake-up call
on the Mir space station
made the same sound as the
emergency alarm.

NASA's tallest astronaut
exceeded their maximum height limit
because he grew taller in space.

In space,
you can relieve a headache
by urinating.

When the waste disposal failed on
the space shuttle *Discovery*,
it developed a giant
urine icicle.

Because their faeces glow in the dark,
lemmings always defecate
underground.

10% of British train toilets
flush directly onto
the tracks.

Before trains had corridors,
ticket inspectors had to clamber along
the outside of the carriage.

More than 20% of people
commuting by train to London
have to stand all the way.

Ⓠ

In the 40 minutes
it takes the average commuter
in the world to get to work,
the ISS travels the distance
from London to Australia.

In the time it takes to
listen to The Proclaimers'
'I'm Gonna Be (500 Miles)',
the ISS travels 500 miles,
then 500 more.

News of the Battle of Trafalgar
travelled the 1,100 miles
to London in 17 days.

In the 17th century,
Christmas turkeys walked from
East Anglia to London
in three months.

The Gombe War (1974–8)
was fought in Tanzania between
two communities of
chimpanzees.

In 1928,
the US, the UK and Germany
signed a treaty to
end all war.

In the Second World War,
the Allies used a 'ghost army'
of inflatable tanks to
trick the Germans.

Stormtroopers from
Star Wars Lego sets
outnumber the planet's
real soldiers by 50 to 1.

The online encyclopaedia
dedicated to Lego is called
'Brickipedia'.

Echolalia
is the urge to imitate
what someone has just said,
in exactly the same voice.

A beauty contest
held in Singapore in 1998
awarded 60% of the marks for
knowledge of the Internet.

Hundreds of victims of the
Great Singapore Penis Panic of 1967
feared their penises were shrinking away;
a dozen of the sufferers
were women.

Men looking at pictures
of two men and a woman produce
more sperm than those looking
at pictures of three women.

Fruit-fly sperm are
20,000 times larger than
porcupine sperm.

The *Pieza* genus of fly
has species called *Pieza kake*,
Pieza pie, *Pieza rhea*
and *Pieza deresistans*.

Reducing the price
of a pizza in France
from €8 to €7.99
increases sales
by 15%.

Pizza sales
shot up in Colorado
after the state legalised
marijuana.

In 1935,
the mayor of New York
banned the sale of artichokes
to ruin a Mafia boss.

In 2010,
the Great Sprout Drought
increased the price per pound of
Brussels sprouts in Britain
almost to that of turkey.

The oldest living turkey
in Britain is called
Dinner.

After noticing that
she washed up bare-handed,
Margaret Thatcher sent the Queen
rubber gloves for Christmas.

The Queen's advisers
persuaded her not to allow
the Loch Ness Monster to be named
Elizabethia nessiae.

The Queen was keen to
accept an offer to be president of
the George Formby Appreciation Society,
but her advisers deemed it
'inappropriate'.

The Queen owns
a drive-thru McDonald's
in Slough.

Because
Chicken McNuggets
are sold in sets of 6, 9 or 20,
the largest number
you *can't* buy
is 43.

People who are
good at maths are
twice as likely to be
sexually active
in old age.

You eat more
when your kitchen
is messy.

Nearly half the seafood
bought in the US is
thrown away.

More fish is eaten in China
than in the following
10 countries
combined.

56 species of fish
can be sold as 'snapper'
in US restaurants.

50 species of microbe
live inside your
belly button.

There are at least
half a million species
of nematode worm
yet to be discovered.

A new fish
discovered in Australia
in 2015 was named
'Blue Bastard'.

The largest land animal
that ever lived was
a dinosaur named
Dreadnoughtus.

After Barack Obama
visited Kenya in 2015,
two women named their sons
Air Force One.

The main street
in the capital of Kosovo is called
Bill Clinton Boulevard.

Bulgaria has
a special agency that
fires anti-hail rockets
into the sky.

Finland has
the highest density
of metal bands in the world.

The unhappiest country
in the world is
Burundi.

Indonesians are
the world's shortest
people.

Pakistanis have
the world's gentlest
handshakes.

The US government spent $7 million
promoting literacy in Pakistan
with an Urdu version of
Sesame Street.

Big Bird,
Bert and Ernie are
the three highest-energy
neutrinos.

The world's
firmest handshakes
belong to the
Swedes.

In 2016,
the Swedish Tourist Association
ran a phone line that you
could call to talk to
a random Swede.

The UN's official definition
of a tourist is someone who stays
in a country more than 24 hours
but less than six months.

The Longquan Buddhist temple in
China has a robotic monk called
Worthy Stupid Robot Monk
designed to talk to tourists.

Items in English on menus in China
include *Fried Swarm*, *The Smell of Urine
Dry Noodles*, *Sauce on My Grandma* and
The Hand that Grasps the Cowboy Bone.

Lifts in Singapore are
fitted with urine detectors;
if triggered, the lift stops and
the police are called.

You are not allowed to
travel in a lift with
liquid nitrogen.

Fear of lifts
can be overcome
by eating all your
meals inside one.

Abibliophobia is
the fear of running out of
something to read.

Sciophobia
is the irrational fear
of shadows.

Steve Jobs
was scared of
buttons.

MC Hammer
doesn't like
hammers.

The Dalai Lama is
frightened of
caterpillars.

Masked birch caterpillars
use 'anal drumming'
to find friends.

People with more friends
have a higher tolerance
for pain.

In Japan,
you can rent
friends.

Hans Christian Andersen
wrecked his friendship with
Charles Dickens by staying
with him three weeks
longer than planned.

Charles Dickens's
father went into business
with Butch Cassidy's
great-grandfather.

The detective agency
that caught Butch Cassidy
also worked for
Coca-Cola.

A can of Coke
uses ingredients from
all seven continents
except Antarctica.

Between 2005 and 2011,
the number of visits to A&E in
the US caused by energy drinks
increased from under 2,000
to over 20,000.

The world's largest cruise ship
has a bar where all the
drinks are made
by robots.

The teabag
was invented 2,000 years
after humans started
drinking tea.

'Night starvation'
was a condition invented
by Horlicks to sell
more Horlicks.

Popcorn
was originally marketed as
Nonpareil.

Noggin
is a protein
that forms the skull.

Bacteria have
the smallest eyeballs
in nature but the largest
relative to their size.

Bees know
when it's going to rain,
so they put in extra work
the day before.

96% of people can
tell the difference between
the sound of hot and cold water
being poured.

The Sandhill Rustic moth
can stay underwater
for an hour.

Sand wasps fly
backwards out of the nest
to make sure they'll remember
what the way home
looks like.

Some spiders
disguise themselves as ants
by pretending their
two front legs are
antennae.

Male spider mites
prefer their sexual partners
to be dead.

Research containing
mathematical formulae is
taken more seriously even
if the formulae are
meaningless.

$$12 + 3 - 4 + 5 + 67 + 8 + 9 = 100$$

20% of British adults
have forgotten how to
calculate percentages.

0111010001100101011001000110
1001011011110111101010101110011
is the digitisation
of the word
'tedious'.

The mathematician Kurt Gödel
lived on a diet of baby food,
laxatives and butter.

'Nutter'
is a type of butter
made from nuts.

The first commercial
suppositories were coated
in cocoa butter.

Lamas in ancient Tibet
were boiled in butter before
being embalmed.

The Ewok language
is a combination of
Tibetan and Nepali.

The British government
advises against travel to Tatooine,
the Tunisian town that inspired
the *Star Wars* planet.

The actors
who played R2-D2 and C-3PO
hated each other.

To build
a real Death Star would
cost $850 million billion.

Venomous frogs
kiss their predators
to death.

A single gram of poison
from Bruno's casque-headed frog
is enough to kill 80 people
or 300,000 mice.

A dead gecko
can stay stuck to the wall
for half an hour.

If an Etruscan shrew
doesn't eat for five hours,
it starves to death.

Elephant shrews, despite
weighing only a few ounces,
are more closely related
to elephants than
to shrews.

Elephants
use their trunks
like leaf blowers to
move food within reach.

Baby elephants
have to be taught
how to use their trunks.

The last time elephants were
used in battle was during
the Iran–Iraq war,
in 1987.

Each archer
at the Battle of Agincourt
had three arrows in the air
at any given moment.

The Battle of Bunker Hill
in fact took place on
Breed's Hill.

The Battle of Waterloo didn't
take place in the village of Waterloo
but in the nearby villages of
Braine l'Alleud and
Plancenoit.

Napoleon
had such painful piles
at the Battle of Waterloo that
he couldn't sit on his horse.

Ulysses S. Grant's
favourite horses were called
Egypt, Cincinnati and
Jeff Davis.

Royal Navy ships' names have
included HMS *Banterer*, HMS *Eclair*,
HMS *Flirt*, HMS *Spanker* and
HMS *Happy Entrance*.

Horatio Nelson's pension
continued to be paid
until 1947.

The US Navy's
'navy blue' uniform
is not blue but black.

The blue-banded bee
head-bangs flowers
350 times a second
to obtain pollen.

Pollen
sticks to bees
by static electricity.

Flea,
the bassist in
the Red Hot Chili Peppers,
keeps over 200,000
bees.

The lifespan
of a rock star
is 25 years shorter
than average.

Mick Jones,
formerly of The Clash,
is a first cousin of Tory MP
Grant Shapps.

The average Briton
has five first cousins,
28 second cousins, 175 third cousins,
1,570 fourth cousins and
17,300 fifth cousins.

The average Briton
has 174,000 sixth cousins,
enough to fill Wembley
stadium twice over.

The average Briton
has two cousins
per square mile.

There is a one in 300 chance
you will be related to a
complete stranger.

In 16th-century Rome,
there was a ban on more than two
sisters from the same family
joining the same convent.

Cloistered nuns
can only leave their
nunnery without permission
in case of fire, leprosy or
contagious illness.

In 1844, French nuns
began meowing like cats,
and only stopped when
the army threatened
to whip them.

In 1841,
Robert Browning
used the word 'twat'
in his poem 'Pippa Passes',
thinking it was an article
of clothing for nuns.

Latin had
about 800 obscene words;
English has only
about 20.

The ancient Romans
told 'Irish' jokes about
people from Thrace.

Ancient Roman
women had no
first names.

From 1850 to 1880,
over 3,000 English women died
after their skirts caught fire.

The most dangerous
household item in a fire
is a fridge-freezer.

Firefighters in Dubai
use jet packs to tackle blazes
in high-rise buildings.

The town of
Centralia, Pennsylvania,
has been on fire
since 1962.

The 1962 escape
from Alcatraz is still
under investigation by
the US Marshals Service.

Before José 'Pepe' Mujica
became president of Uruguay,
he spent 14 years in prison,
two of them locked
in a horse trough.

If the US freed all its prisoners
except murderers and rapists,
it would still have more
people in prison
per head than
Germany.

1 in 6 of the world's population
bribe a police officer every year.

Because of a deal struck with
the Mafia, the word 'mafia' was
never used in *The Godfather*.

Half the world's population
has seen a Bond movie.

Mice prefer watching
violent mouse movies
to erotic ones.

4-year-old mice
are much rarer than
100-year-old people.

One of the longest
domain names in the world is:
iamtheproudownerofthelongestlongest
longestdomainnameinthisworld.com

The longest
human pregnancy lasted
a year and 10 days.

A million seconds
is 11.6 days.

A billion seconds
is 32 years.

3.8 billion years ago,
a day was less than
10 hours long.

The Sex Pistols' debut album
is closer in time to the premiere of
Rachmaninoff's Third Symphony
than it is to today.

The last note of
The Beatles' 'A Day in the Life'
is so high that only
dogs can hear it.

Wrens
can sing 36 notes
a second.

Over its lifetime,
an Arctic tern flies the equivalent
of three trips to the Moon
and back.

Ancient murrelets
are birds that migrate
16,000 miles from Canada to Japan
and back for no good reason:
conditions are identical
in both places.

Anthropologists
can track human migration
by examining earwax.

There are only
140 cases in medical history of
a man having more than
two testicles.

The last
two journalists
to work in Fleet Street
left in 2016.

Betteridge's Law of Headlines
states that a headline ending in a
question mark can always be
answered 'No'.

There is no evidence that the headline
'Heavy Fog in Channel – Continent Cut Off'
ever ran in a British newspaper.

A 2013 study of
Fox News's climate-science reports
found that 72% were
misleading.

When weather forecasting started,
the ship-salvage industry
tried to get it banned.

The world's longest ship
is 50% longer than
the Shard is tall.

London gets
less rain than Rome,
Venice or Nice.

Britons spend
five months of their lives
complaining about
the weather.

Plothering
is a Midlands word
for a heavy downpour.

Sólarfrí
is Icelandic for
time off given to staff to
enjoy good weather.

Physiggoomai
is ancient Greek for a
person who is aroused
by garlic.

French
has no word for
'shrug'.

A *sciolist*
is someone who
knows less than
they pretend.

To *snudge*
is to stride around
pretending to look busy.

Sinapistic means
'consisting of mustard'.

Subrident
means
'smiling'.

One person produces
enough urine in a lifetime
to fill a swimming pool.

Before becoming
a Founding Father,
Benjamin Franklin considered
becoming a swimming teacher.

In 1958,
Chairman Mao
invited Khrushchev
to a swimming meeting,
knowing that he couldn't swim.
Khrushchev had to wear armbands.

There are Egyptian cave paintings
of people doing breaststroke.

The first man
to swim the English Channel
later toured a show where
he floated in a tank
for 128 hours.

The number of hours
that Britons spent watching
The One Show in 2015 is greater
than the number of hours that
have passed since humans
first left Africa.

During the launch of BBC2 in 1964,
a kangaroo got stuck in a lift
at Television Centre.

For the Queen's coronation in 1953,
people dressed up
as TV sets.

In 1940s Britain,
children's TV was
shown from 5 to 6 p.m.,
then transmission stopped
for an hour to encourage
them to go to bed.

After the introduction of colour TV,
the number of people dreaming
in black and white fell
from 25% to 7%.

Nightmares
are more common
if you sleep on your
left-hand side.

When you sleep
in a bed for the first time,
half of your brain
stays awake.

Women sleep
half an hour longer
than men.

Netflix has
created a pair of socks that
pause the show you're watching
if you fall asleep.

1 in 5 people
wake up wearing
fewer items of clothing
than they went
to bed in.

Follicle mites
make the journey across
a sleeping person's face
from nose to ear
in six hours.

The DNA in your facial mites can
tell scientists where you came from.

The first passport-holders
had to provide written descriptions
of themselves instead of photos.
Nearly everyone described
their noses as
'average'.

To qualify for
a Dutch passport,
you have to watch a video
showing beach nudity.

Godzilla
was awarded
Japanese citizenship
in 2015.

Prospective
citizens of South Korea
must sing the first four verses
of the national anthem.

In 2014,
South Korea changed the key
of its national anthem to
make it easier
to sing.

Until 1857,
all British passports were
signed by the Foreign Secretary.

Q

Until 1858,
all British passports
were written in French.

In the 1880s,
the French used half
as much soap as
the English.

In 19th-century France,
it was a symbol of free thinking
to hold a sausage-eating party
on Good Friday.

In 1955,
America had
a 'Sausage Queen'
beauty contest.

The man who
first described Botox
was a German known as
'Sausage' Kerner.

Germans who
urinate in the street
are known as
Wildpinkler.

The best day to find money
in the streets of New York City
is 18 March: the day after
St Patrick's Day.

New York's ants
clean up the streets by
eating the equivalent of
60,000 hot dogs
every year.

In 'Find the Lady',
the man who mixes up
the cards is known as
'the Tosser'.

If a flatworm can't find
another flatworm to mate with,
it stabs itself in the head
with its own penis.

Male nematode worms
have an extra pair of brain cells,
which are thought to help
them to remember
to have sex.

Nematode worms
use slugs as taxis to
carry them around.

The average
Bentley driver owns
eight cars.

The average
Bugatti driver owns
84 cars, three jets and
a yacht.

For the last 70 years,
the average price of a small car
has remained the same as the cost
of 20,000 Mars Bars.

Driving a car to Mars
would emit as much carbon as
there is in all the trees
in Edinburgh.

Overdrafts,
digestive biscuits
and the hypodermic syringe
were all invented in Edinburgh.

The Bank of England was
founded by a Scotsman
in 1694.

The Bank of Scotland was
founded by an Englishman
in 1695.

The first Nando's
opened in London
in 1696.

More people
live in London than in
Scotland and Wales
combined.

London has
more trees than
any capital city
in Europe.

Every English elm is
descended from a single tree
imported by the Romans.

It would take 300 years to
catalogue all the tree species
in the Amazon rainforest.

The world has lost
3% of its forests
since 1990.

A 106-acre
aspen forest in Utah
is made up of a single
80,000-year-old tree.

No matter how large a tree is,
it will break if the wind speed
reaches 94 mph.

Trees sleep at night
to rest their
branches.

Mags Thomson
of Livingston, Scotland,
has spent 21 years trying
to visit all the branches
of Wetherspoons.

Tony Blair
was the first serving
British prime minister to
visit California.

The California gull
is the state bird
of Utah.

When Memphis, Tennessee, held
a 'Dinosaurs Live' exhibition in 1992,
visitors demanded refunds
because the dinosaurs
weren't alive.

Americans are 22 times
more likely to be killed
by a cow than by
a shark.

There are more
gun shops in the US than
Starbucks, McDonald's
and supermarkets
put together.

Bosnia
has one betting shop
for every 1,000 people.

Rats
will gamble more if
a win is accompanied by
flashing lights and
a fanfare.

Q

A sloth's top speed is
six centimetres
a second.

Shakespeare's plays have
seven times more roles
for men than women.

Britons apologise at least
eight times a day.

Chinese drivers
are stuck in traffic jams
for the equivalent of
nine days a year.

People are 39% more likely
to buy the brand of car
their parents owned.

In 8th-century England,
it was a sin for a man
to see his wife
naked.

In 1870,
Windsor Baths
were moved because
naked men could be seen
from Queen Victoria's bedroom.

A painting of a half-naked couple in a
Sydney bathroom has been shared
by more than a million people
as the perfect depiction
of modern marriage.

To take a bath with
electricity running through it
was a 19th-century cure
for rheumatism.

According to a 2013 survey,
3% of Londoners regularly
eat in the bath.

If the Earl of Sandwich had
got the earldom he really wanted,
we'd all be eating
portsmouths.

Restaurants
in New Zealand
that sell cooked locusts
advertise them as
'sky prawns'.

The first-ever
skywriting message was
an advert which said
'DAILY MAIL'.

The Wright brothers had
a joint bank account.

The UK's
national sperm bank
has just nine donors.

In 2014,
nine children in the US
were named
Chaos.

Himalayan Ascent,
a Nepalese mountain-guide company,
was founded by a climber
called Sumit.

The Erasmus Medical Centre
in Rotterdam has a
urologist called
Dik Kok.

The British judge
whose report led to all
cigarette packaging being green
is Mr Justice Green.

A man arrested
in 2015 for trespassing at
the Budweiser brewery in St Louis
was called Bud Weisser.

Once Brewed
is a village in
Northumberland
also known as
Twice Brewed.

Bouth,
a village in Cumbria,
is not pronounced
'Bowth' or 'Booth'
but 'Both'.

In 1876, a man was shot
because of an argument over
the correct way to pronounce
'Newfoundland'.

Labradors
come from Newfoundland,
not Labrador.

The 'California roll'
was invented in Canada,
not California.

Oceanographers in California
collect spray from whales' blowholes
using drones known
as 'snot bots'.

Whales can suffocate
if fish get stuck in their
blowholes.

Dolphins
have blowhole
sex.

Peacocks
fake orgasm noises
to trick peahens into
thinking they're more
sexually active.

Stick insects
can be stuck together
having sex for
79 days.

Moths
can remember the
species of plant they
first had sex on.

Plants
are able to forget
stressful experiences.

The number
of messages sent
every two days via
WhatsApp and Facebook
exceeds the number of
human beings who
have ever lived.

The numbers
on a roulette wheel
add up to 666.

It would take
more than 65,000
tweets to write out Proust's
À la recherche du temps perdu.

Brazil has
more mobile phones
than people.

In 2013,
a Florida law
accidentally banned
computers.

You can't write
perfect French on French
computer keyboards.

In 1861,
only 2.5% of Italians
could speak Italian.

70% of Italians imagine
that life is good in France, but
only 43% of the French
agree with them.

The term *nom de plume*
is not French.

The French
rire dans sa barbe
('to laugh in one's beard')
means 'to chuckle quietly
about a past event'.

The Croatian for
'what goes around comes around'
is *doće maca na vratanca* –
'the pussy cat will come
to the tiny door'.

The German for
not seeing the blindingly obvious
is *Tomaten auf den Augen haben* –
'to have tomatoes
on the eyes'.

In Germany, it is
illegal to wear a mask
or take a pillow to
a demonstration.

17th-century Germans
were banned from wearing
very wide trousers.

Monty Python's Life of Brian
was banned by several UK councils
that didn't have cinemas.

Divorce
was illegal in Ireland
until 1997.

In 1457,
men with moustaches
were banned from
Dublin.

De befborstel
is a moustache
grown by Dutchmen
to stimulate the clitoris.

The Ainu people of Japan
wear wooden moustache lifters
to keep their facial hair
out of their food.

The world's longest beard
is 16 feet long and kept at
the Smithsonian Museum.

The Kansas
Barbed Wire Museum
has 2,000 varieties
of barbed wire.

The Pencil Sharpener Museum
in Logan, Ohio, has 3,400
pencil sharpeners.

The Museo della Merda
in Piacenza, Italy, is the world's
first museum dedicated
to excrement.

Proctologists
in ancient Egypt were known as
'shepherds of the anus'.

Ⓠ

Ancient Egyptians
believed the purpose of the brain
was to produce snot
for the nose.

Cured pork
inserted into the nostrils
can stop nosebleeds.

85% of people
use only one nostril
at a time.

One nostril
smells the world
slightly differently
to the other.

Sea hares
are molluscs that
secrete a purple slime to
block their predators'
sense of smell.

Puff adders
can 'switch off'
their own smell so
predators can't locate them.

Orang-utans
warn off predators
by making kissing noises.

Fewer than half
of modern cultures
practise romantic kissing.

The highwayman
Jerry Abershawe
went to the gallows
with a flower in his mouth.

'Hanging days',
when criminals were executed
in Georgian London,
were public holidays.

The head of the police
in ancient Egypt was known as
the 'chief of the hitters'.

British police officers
are arrested for criminal behaviour
at a rate of one a day.

Cambodian traffic police
pocket 70% of all the
fines they collect.

The first recorded traffic casualty
was a Roman pig run over
by a chariot carrying an
ornamental phallus.

The first police-car chase
in the UK had a
top speed of
15 mph.

Russia has
enough miles of road to
go from the Earth to the Moon,
circle it 15 times,
and come back.

Vodka was
banned in Russia
between 1914 and 1925.

Gin
was voted
'best drink of 1873'.

In 2013,
Heineken adverts
inadvertently featured a
19th-century anti-alcohol crusader.

John Wesley,
the founder of Methodism,
cured his overeating by poking a piece
of wine-soaked bread
up his nose.

Winston Churchill's doctor
prescribed eight double shots
of alcohol per day.

Churchill
was a US citizen.

12% of Americans think
USB is a country
in Europe.

31% of Americans
believe they have made
contact with
the dead.

1 in 3 adults
in the US own
at least one gun.

Utah, Arizona, Indiana,
West Virginia, Pennsylvania
and Alaska all have official
state firearms.

The largest university in Texas
allows handguns on campus,
but not water pistols.

After arms and drugs,
the third most smuggled
commodity is
animals.

The world's slavery trade
is worth $150 billion a year,
more than the GDP of
Hungary.

More people
work for Walmart
than live in
Slovenia.

Bolivia
has had 190 coups
or revolutions in its
191-year history.

There is only
one psychiatrist
in Liberia.

Liberia declared
a state of emergency in 2009
when 80 towns and villages
were invaded by
caterpillars.

The Very
Hungry Caterpillar
was originally called
A Week with Willie Worm.

The gum-leaf
skeletoniser caterpillar
of Australia wears a stack of
its old moulted heads
on its head.

When Donald Trump
is in a bad mood, he
wears a red hat.

The English philosopher
Herbert Spencer had an
'angry suit' which he wore
when feeling irritable.

The phrase
'survival of the fittest'
was coined by Herbert Spencer,
not Charles Darwin.

The repetition of
a falsehood so often it
becomes an urban legend
is known as the
Woozle Effect.

WIMPs and WIMPZILLAs
are theoretical particles
made of theoretical
'dark matter'.

46% of Americans
feel a deep sense of wonder
about the universe at least
once a week.

Valentina Tereshkova,
the first woman in space,
forgot her toothbrush and
had to brush her teeth
with her finger.

Napoleon
was born with
teeth.

Limpet teeth
are made from the
strongest biological
material in nature.

When Monty Python
toured the US and were asked to
trash a hotel suite for publicity,
Michael Palin obligingly went
into the bathroom and
broke a toothbrush.

Pythons kill
not by suffocation, but by
cutting off the blood supply
and causing a heart attack.

A human heart
beats five times as often
in a lifetime as a
giraffe's.

Fatal heart attacks
can be caused
by joy.

Having friendly neighbours
reduces your chances
of a heart attack
by up to 70%.

In 1996,
two neighbours in Devon
spent a year hooting at owls,
unaware they were actually
hooting at each other.

'The Copper-Penis Owl' is
the monster used in Hungary
to scare children into
behaving.

Children in Hungary are
told that eating carrots
will help them
whistle.

A mussel
from Transylvania
that lives in toilet U-bends
is the UK's most invasive species.

A supplement
made from mussels
can reduce the pain
in your muscles.

The muscles in the
left ventricle of a giraffe's heart
are five times stronger than
those in the right.

There are
half as many giraffes
as there were
15 years
ago.

The producer
of *Die Hard* and *The Matrix*
also invented the sport of
Ultimate Frisbee.

The sound of the stabbing
in the shower scene in *Psycho*
was made using melons.

Nobody knows
why the Oscars are
called the Oscars.

Cary Grant and Clark Gable
met once a year to exchange
unwanted monogrammed
Christmas gifts.

Christmas-tree lights
can interfere with
your Wi-Fi.

Siberian Christmas trees
get so cold they can
turn to glass.

Pine-tree needles
are a good source of
vitamins A and C.

Pine-tree sap
was used in the
Second World War
to fuel Japanese aircraft.

85% of aircraft that crashed on
British soil during the Second World War
belonged to the Allies.

Soldiers in
the First World War
were five times more likely
to get venereal disease
than trench foot.

M&Ms were invented
so American soldiers could
eat chocolate without it
melting in their hands.

In 2013,
70,000 tons more chocolate
were consumed than
the cocoa harvest
produced.

Cocoa trees belong
to the *Sterculiaceae* family,
which is named after the
Roman god of manure.

Sgriob is Gaelic for
'the itchiness that overcomes the
upper lip just before taking
a sip of whisky'.

Cravings for
chocolate and alcohol
can be controlled with
injections of lizard saliva.

Osteria Francescana,
voted the world's best restaurant in 2016,
has a dish on the menu called
'the crunchy part of
the lasagna'.

Not supplying trays in cafeterias
reduces food waste by 32%.

In 2016,
Thailand's Buddhist monks
were put on a diet after a survey
revealed almost half of them
were obese.

In 1087,
William the Conqueror
got too fat to ride his horse,
so he went on an alcohol-only diet
and died later that year.

You get
18% more drunk if
you drink spirits with
a diet mixer rather than
a regular one.

Hens
given alcohol
lay half as many eggs.

Human beings produce
1,000,000,000,000,000,000,000,000,000
times more sperm
than eggs.

The sperm of
a male seed shrimp
are three times bigger
than he is.

The oldest known sperm
is worm sperm.

A newly discovered
'100-suckered parasitic worm'
turned out to be the genitals of
the blanket octopus.

Gloomy octopuses
are said to have
'no personality'.

Octopuses
prefer HDTV to
ordinary television.

Squidward Tentacles
in *SpongeBob SquarePants* has
only six tentacles – which means
he is neither a squid
nor an octopus.

@

The most
remote point
on Earth is called
Point Nemo.

The hottest place on Earth
lost the title it had held for 90 years
in 2012, when it was found that the man
making the original measurements
didn't know how to use a
thermometer.

The Sun is white
(with a hint of turquoise),
not yellow.

Man has probed
20 billion kilometres
outwards from the Earth
but only 12 into it.

Aboard the
NASA probe
sent to study Pluto
were the ashes of the man
who discovered it.

Astronauts
aboard the ISS
change their underpants
every four days.

Astronauts wear belts
to stop their trousers
falling up.

Astronauts have to
sleep near fans so they don't
suffocate in their own
exhaled breath.

Astronauts
drink their own
recycled urine.

In 2015, a whisky sent
into space to mature was said
to taste of antiseptic smoke,
rubber and smoked fish.

On Earth,
moss grows in
an unruly fashion, but
in space it forms
spirals.

If you grow
romaine lettuce in space,
it tastes like rocket.

There are 400,000
species of plants on Earth.
300,000 are safe to eat, but
actually we only eat
fewer than 200.

In winter, garden birds
need to eat a third of their
own weight in food
each day.

Paradisea apoda,
the 'legless bird of paradise', is
so named because the original specimen's
legs were cut off when it was
being stuffed.

An Australian dentist
has invented braces for
birds with bent beaks.

A flock
of red-billed queleas
may consist of over
30 million birds.

Until the 1840s,
rugby matches could have
up to 300 players on
the pitch at once.

Estádio Milton Corrêa,
a football stadium in Brazil, has
one goal in the northern hemisphere
and one in the southern hemisphere.

The British Ladies Football Club
was founded in 1895 by
Nettie Honeyball.

The first black
female footballer was
Carrie Boustead, a Scot who
played in goal in
the 1890s.

In 2015, Welling United
signed a promising young
Chelsea player called
Nortei Nortey.

A scientific paper published in 2016
had over 2,000 authors, including
38 Wangs, 3 Dings, 3 Dongs,
a Botti and a Brest.

At least 200
medical papers
quote Bob Dylan
in their titles.

Fraudulent
scientific papers
tend to contain
more jargon.

When walking,
anxious people tend to
veer to the left.

Penguins
have a 'slender walk'
where they pin their flippers back
to wriggle through crowds.

Penguins
prepare a warm spot on
the ground to lay their eggs
by excreting all over it.

Fat penguins
fall over more often than
thin ones.

New Zealand has
more species of penguin
than anywhere else.

Jackass penguins are
named after their mating cry
and are sometimes known
as 'beach donkeys'.

An 18th-century name
for penguins was
'arse-feet'.

The feet of
tree frogs are
self-cleaning.

For Spider-Man
to climb buildings like a gecko
would require size 89 feet.

Humans
started wearing shoes
40,000 years ago.

Socrates had
a disciple called
Simon the Shoemaker.

Wellington boots were
designed by Germans,
named by an Irishman,
manufactured by an American
and first worn by French peasants.

Wearing your socks
outside your shoes gives you
a better grip in icy weather.

The first water balloons
were made out of socks.

The word 'sock'
comes from the Latin *soccus*,
meaning 'shoe'.

The word 'pants' comes
from a Greek word meaning
'all-compassionate'.

The word 'sarcasm' comes
from an ancient Greek verb
meaning 'to tear flesh'.

The name Bryony comes
from the Greek verb *bruein*,
meaning 'to be full to bursting'.

Spartan elections
were won by the candidate
who got the loudest cheer.

The loudest word
ever shouted was 'Quiet!'
by a primary-school teacher
from Northern Ireland.

In 2009,
Jonathan Lee Riches
served an injunction on
Guinness World Records
to stop them calling him the
'world's most litigious person'.

The record for the world's
fastest steam train was set in 1938
and has never been broken.

When France's TGV
broke the world train-speed record,
it had to apply the brakes for
10 miles before stopping.

Japanese railways
have underpasses
for turtles.

Tartle
is an old Scottish word for
the moment of panic when you're
about to introduce someone and
realise you've forgotten
their name.

In 1963,
5,529 Nigels were
born in England and Wales;
in 2014, there were
only 10.

Men called Nigel
are twice as likely to
vote for UKIP.

In a 2015 poll,
30% of Republicans
and 19% of Democrats
supported the bombing of Agrabah,
the fictional city
in *Aladdin*.

The 25th Amendment,
allowing vice presidents to take over
when the president is incapacitated,
has been used only three times.
In each case, the president
was having a colonoscopy.

George H. W. Bush
almost chose Clint Eastwood
as his running mate.

The name Donald means
'ruler of the world'.

Donald Trump's
father and grandmother both had
the middle name Christ.

The Virgin Mary
appears more often
in the Qur'an than
in the Bible.

To print a single
Gutenberg Bible on vellum
required the hides
of 170 calves.

Parchment
is made from the skin
of sheep.

The parchment scroll of the
Land Tax Act of 1782
is a quarter of a
mile long.

The first use of
the word 'twat' in Parliament
was in 1986, when Bill Cash MP
described Field Marshal Lord Carver
as a 'boring old twat'.

The second use
of 'twat' in Parliament
happened immediately afterwards,
when another MP shouted:
'He said twat!'

According to Hansard, no MP
has ever called another MP a 'turd'.

MPs have been told
not to stroke the statues
in Parliament for luck because
Churchill and Thatcher are
being worn away.

A statue
of Nikola Tesla in
Silicon Valley provides
free Wi-Fi.

The Statue of Liberty was
designed as a Muslim woman
guarding the Suez Canal.

For almost 40 years,
Stockton-on-Tees honoured John Walker,
the inventor of the friction match,
with a statue of the wrong man.

The man who patented
the first elevator and the man
who patented the first elevator brake
were both called Otis.

Crohn's disease
was discovered and named by
Marilyn Monroe's doctor.

Because of
mad cow disease
Desperate Dan stopped
eating cow pie.

Until 1899,
the list of official diseases of
the Royal College of Physicians
included nostalgia.

The US government's
Centers for Disease Control and Prevention
provide specific guidance for
Zombie Preparedness.

A group
of unicorns
is called a blessing.

'Unicorn Zombie Apocalypse'
comes with an official
music video.

50% of Americans
believe in at least one
conspiracy theory.

95% of
people on Earth
have at least one thing
wrong with them.

In 1942,
half of the US's
penicillin stocks were
used on just one patient.

According to at least two
independent sets of research,
man flu is real.

In 1873, three-quarters
of American horses
caught flu.

In 2015,
the Queen received
a gift of £5,000 worth of
horse semen.

A champion racehorse
from today would beat one
from the early 1990s
by seven lengths.

Victorian gentry
ordered their horses to be
shot after their deaths.

'Twitter'
was a 19th-century
word for an abscess on
on a horse's foot.

All the photos
shared on Snapchat
in one hour would take
10 years to view.

People
who use more emoji
have more sex.

Emoji is the
fastest-growing
language in history.

72% of
18- to 25-year-olds
find it easier to express their feelings
with emoji rather than words.

The average Briton is
bored for six hours
a week.

One British child a day
eats a washing-machine tablet
in mistake for a sweet.

The average Briton's
wardrobe contains 152 items,
fewer than half of which
are worn regularly.

One-third of Britons have
written almost nothing by hand
in the last six months.

Lord Baden-Powell
once wrote a letter to an
autograph-hunter telling him not
to become an autograph-hunter.
It has since been sold to
an autograph-hunter.

As a small boy,
Roald Dahl made a
pilgrimage to see Beatrix Potter.
When he got there, all she said was:
'Well, you've seen her. Now, buzz off!'

The Oompa-Loompas
were originally called
Whipple-Scrumpets.

The Girl with the Dragon Tattoo is
how the author Stieg Larsson imagined
Pippi Longstocking as an adult.

The video game *Fallout 4*
is set in a post-apocalyptic world
where you get rewarded for
returning library books.

In his lifetime,
Edgar Allan Poe's
best-selling book was
a textbook about seashells.

Ernest Hemingway
held the world record for
the most marlin caught
in a single day.

Marcel Proust
had opium for
breakfast.

People who
drink black coffee
are more likely to be
psychopaths.

Drinking coffee
in the Ottoman Empire
of the 17th century
was punishable
by death.

The Venetians
used biological warfare
against the Ottomans by
smearing plague pus
on fezzes.

The beehive hairdo
was invented to
fit under a fez.

It is illegal in
Tajikistan to go out for
a birthday meal.

In China,
it's illegal to
reincarnate without
filling in a government
Reincarnation Application form.

In 2011,
Florida accidentally
made sex illegal.

Until 1936,
it was illegal for
men in New York
to be topless in public.

After the English Civil War,
Quakers appeared naked in public
to symbolise the shame of the
Church of England.

Keen nudists have included
Benjamin Franklin, Walt Whitman,
Dr Seuss, Dame Helen Mirren
and Billy Connolly.

America's first streaker
rose to become chief clerk
of the Pension Bureau.

In July 1896,
a man called George Bush was
sent to prison for appearing naked in
a first-class railway carriage.

When George H. W. Bush
arrived in the White House, he found
a note from Ronald Reagan saying:
'Don't let the turkeys
get you down.'

Ronald Reagan left a note
on the White House lawn warning
the squirrels to beware of
George H. W. Bush's dogs.

'The Catman' plagued
Ronald Reagan with threatening letters
and dozens of pictures of cats.

Abraham Lincoln
received at least one
threatening letter
every day of his
presidency.

The Royal Mail
has calculated that
it would cost £11,602.25
to send a letter to Mars.

75% of the
Earth's population has
no postal address.

The first woman
to appear on a US postage stamp
was Queen Isabella of Spain.

The second item
sent by New York's
pneumatic-tube postal system
was a live black cat.

Ducklings
are capable of
abstract thought.

Every year,
British ducks are fed
3.5 million loaves
of bread.

In the California Gold Rush,
a slice of bread cost the
equivalent of $25,
or $50 if it was
buttered.

The ancient Romans
had a special kind of bread
to be eaten with oysters.

When the ancient Romans
deployed lions against Germanic tribes,
the tribesmen simply assumed
they were large dogs.

The first successful CPR
was performed
on a dog.

Lancashire
is haunted by a
ghostly dog called
the 'Radcliffe shag'.

10% of
vegetarian hot dogs in
America contain
meat.

A 'sandwich' in
the US must legally be
at least 35% cooked meat.

Commercially grown
tomatoes have tripled in size
since the 1970s.

In the mid–1980s, the
National Giant Vegetable Championships
had to move to a new venue because
the pumpkins were getting too big
to fit through the door.

The world's heaviest pumpkin
weighed the same as
a Ford Fiesta.

Americans eat
20% of their meals
in cars.

Cucumbers are
sometimes sacrificed by the
Nuer people of South Sudan
as a substitute for
cattle.

Every year,
250,000 Danes gather
to watch cows being
let out to pasture.

Until the 1950s,
the rural poor in Norway
warmed their feet
in cowpats.

Cows produce
five times as much
saliva as milk.

To stop their
udders freezing
Siberian cows
wear bras.

Cartoon cows
in 1930s Hollywood
were not allowed udders.

'Cowabunga!'
was used by Snoopy long before the
Teenage Mutant Ninja Turtles.

In 2000,
Blockbuster Video
turned down the chance to acquire
a new video-streaming service
called Netflix.

The original Chill Pill
was a pill that you took
when you had a chill.

In the 16th century,
'to text' meant
'to quote texts'.

In 1994,
people said 'marvellous'
77 times as often as
they do today.

Pilots never say 'Over and out' because
'over' means 'waiting to hear more'
and 'out' means 'that's the end
of the conversation'.

Anyone talking on an army radio
should be careful not to use
the word 'repeat' because
it means 'fire again'.

In the Second World War,
the group trying to 'turn' German spies
was called the Twenty Committee, hence
the 'XX' or 'Double Cross' Committee.

Major Edwin Richardson,
who ran the British War Dog School,
was prepared to accept any dog
as long as it didn't have
a 'gaily carried tail'.

'Dalmatian'
is from an ancient
Illyrian word meaning
'sheep'.

America's
'National Hero Dog' award
was won in 2015
by a cat.

Galeanthropy is
the belief that you have
become a cat.

In 1954,
the Soviet Union
applied to join NATO.

President Kennedy wanted
the first three men on the Moon
to be white, black and Asian.

The first song
played on the Moon
was 'Fly Me to the Moon'.

In 1966,
three years before
the US put a man on the Moon,
a spacecraft from the USSR
reached Venus.

On the anniversary
of its landing on Mars,
the *Curiosity* rover hummed
'Happy Birthday' to itself.

NASA scientists
working on Mars rovers
work to a Mars day,
not an Earth day.

In 20 million years,
Mars's moon Phobos
will have disintegrated into
a ring around the planet.

The Earth seen from
the Moon never seems
to rise or set but just
hangs in the sky.

When a potential meteorite
turns out to be just a rock,
geologists call it a
'meteorwrong'.

In the past 50 years,
humanity has mined
enough rock to fill
the Grand Canyon
to the brim.

'Rock 'n' roll'
originally meant
the waves of fervour in
US gospel churches.

The Church of England has
four and a half times as
many buildings in
the UK as Tesco.

'Noon'
used to be
the ninth hour
of the religious day
and took place at 3 p.m.

Wythnos,
the Welsh for 'week',
means 'eight nights'.

In Anglo-Saxon times,
the day began
at sunset.

In Saudi Arabia,
the first day of the week
is Saturday.

In Ethiopia,
the millennium fell on
12 September 2007.

There is
no standard day
on which to celebrate
World Standards Day.

World Health Day and
America's National Beer Day
are both on 7 April.

The US celebrates
National Cheeseburger Day
on 18 September.

In the 16th century,
unwanted fat was
called 'fog'.

The only difference
between fog and mist is
visibility: if you can't see more
than 100 metres ahead, it's fog, not mist.

'Thunder-plump'
is an old Scottish word
for a sudden heavy rain shower.

Wabsteid,
cauldpress and *stoor-sooker*
are recent Scots words for
'website', 'fridge' and
'vacuum cleaner'.

Scatophagus argus is a fish
whose Latin name means
'many-eyed shit-eater',
so it's politely called
the 'spotted scat'.

There is a
butterfly species called
Charis matic.

Han solo is
the scientific name of a
450-million-year-old
trilobite.

Most 'Latin'
scientific names
aren't really Latin.

Half of
all museum specimens
are thought to be
wrongly labelled.

A collection of felt hats
in the V&A Museum in London were
made using mercury and are stored
in special bags marked with
a skull and crossbones.

The whale skeleton at the
Natural History Museum in London
is held together by papier mâché
made from 80-year-old copies
of the *Kent Messenger*.

The world's only
Cornish-pasty museum
is in Mexico.

Mushrooms
shoot spores into the air
to make it rain.

When the Moon
is directly overhead,
its gravity pulls on clouds
and makes it rain less.

'Flisk' is an old
Gloucestershire word
for a light shower.

Scientists can tell
how much it rained
two billion years ago.

The Sun is rained on
by droplets of plasma
the size of Ireland.

In one hour,
the Sun produces as much energy
as the world's population
uses in a year.

The energy used in a year by
Britons charging their phones
would be enough to power
Birmingham and Bradford.

In 2011,
a skydiver dropped
an iPhone from 13,500 feet
and it still worked.

There are only
five full-time skywriters
on Earth.

There are
13,513 airports in the US,
more than the next 12 countries
put together.

In 2013/14,
only eight passengers
used the railway station
at Teesside Airport.

The French for 'airport novel'
is *roman de gare*, or
'railway station
novel'.

H. G. Wells
was A. A. Milne's
maths teacher.

Marlon Brando's mother
gave Henry Fonda
acting lessons.

Roald Dahl, Noël Coward, Greta Garbo,
Cary Grant, Frank Sinatra, Harry Houdini
and Christopher Lee all
worked as spies.

Errol Flynn was
a Nazi sympathiser and
wrote letters to Hitler.

The average human being
is significantly more dangerous
than the average sociopath.

Even before farming was invented,
humans had killed over half
the planet's large
mammals.

There is no known case
of an invasive species causing
the extinction of a plant.

Species
that have disappeared
from Britain in the last 200 years
include the black-backed meadow ant,
the short-haired bumblebee,
the tawny earwig and
the rooting puffball.

The Morro Bay kangaroo rat
of California is probably extinct.
It hasn't been seen in the wild
for 30 years, and the last one
in captivity died in 1993.

The name of the kangaroo mouse,
Microdipodops megacephalus,
means 'two small feet
with a big head'.

Baby sabre-toothed cats
had sabre baby teeth.

Slugs have
approximately
27,000 teeth.

Britain has
230 slugs for
every human.

Belgium is the
world's leading exporter
of billiard balls.

All the Cadbury's Crunchies
in Europe are made
in Poland.

More than 4,000
different varieties of potato
are grown in Peru.

The US has an
awards ceremony called
'Potato Man of the Year'.

Las Vegas
hosts an awards ceremony for
people who make awards.

At the first
modern Olympics in 1896,
the medals for winners
were silver.

Philip Noel-Baker MP
is the only person ever to have been
awarded both an Olympic medal (1920)
and a Nobel Prize (1959).

Princess Diana
won a prize at school for
Best Kept Guinea Pig.

Man Group,
sponsors of the Booker Prize,
were once responsible for supplying
the Royal Navy's rum ration.

During the Second World War,
US Navy sailors were given
detailed instructions on
what to do if caught
by a giant clam.

The Royal Navy's
most advanced destroyer
breaks if it sails into
warm water.

The Royal Navy uses
a version of Windows XP called
'Windows for Submarines'.

The wardrooms in
Russian nuclear submarines are
clad in stainless steel and have
a sauna and a plunge pool.

The wardrooms in
French nuclear submarines are
done out in panelled wood
and have a fish tank.

British nuclear submarines
have their wardrooms fitted out
with Formica, because it's
less of a fire risk.

North Korea has
10 times as many
submarines as
Britain.

North Korea has
eight Internet hosts;
the US has
505 million.

Marijuana
is legal in
North Korea.

Marijuana has
never been illegal
in Uruguay.

Smoking marijuana
increases a person's
appetite by 40%.

Meerkats have
competitive eating contests
to establish dominance.

Feral cats in Australia eat
75 million native animals
every day.

From 1840 to 1930,
a pod of killer whales helped
South Australian whalers kill
baleen whales in return for
being given their lips and
tongues to eat.

The excrement of
sperm whales is worth
up to $10,000
a pound.

In the Middle Ages,
people slept with cow dung
at the foot of their bed
to keep bugs away.

In the Middle Ages,
bras were called
'breastbags'.

A bra
has been invented
that doubles as
a gas mask.

A gas station
owned by Harland Sanders
was the site of the first KFC in 1930.
Motorists were served fried chicken
at his own dining-room table.

Napoleon
loved roast chicken
and made sure his chefs
had one on the spit
at all hours.

Meat from scared animals
is tougher and less tasty.

The carnivorous harp sponge
traps prey in the grille of its body,
then dissolves it
cell by cell.

One bite from
the lone star tick can
make you allergic
to red meat.

Beaver tail
tastes like
roast beef.

Jellyfish contain
the same number of calories
as green tea.

Antarctic silverfish are pink.
They only turn silver
when they die.

Silverfish
drink by sucking moist air
in through their anus.

Tap water in
Windhoek, Namibia,
tastes salty because 25% of it
is recycled sewage.

After water,
the most widely
consumed food or drink
on Earth is tea.

In the Second World War,
tea was moved out of London
to keep it safe.

The 'WD' in WD40
stands for 'Water Displacement';
the '40' is there because the
inventor took 40 goes
to get it right.

The inventor of
sociology also invented
the Body Mass Index.

You're more likely to order
dessert in a restaurant
if your waiter is
overweight.

At an all-you-can-eat restaurant,
men who eat with women
eat twice as much as
men who dine
with men.

Voles eat 80%
of their own weight
every day.

Grey squirrels
can digest acorns;
red squirrels
can't.

The RSPB recommends
sprinkling chilli on bird food
to deter squirrels because
birds can't taste it but
squirrels can.

Squirrels pretend
to hide their nuts
to fool potential thieves.

Jays 'weigh' nuts in the shell
by shaking them and listening to
the noise they make.

Nuts in their shells
don't attract VAT but
shelled nuts do.

VAT
is payable on
ornamental vegetables
but not on culinary
vegetables.

In the 18th century,
Britain had a tax
on wallpaper.

From 1796–1847,
the British responded to
a tax on dog's tails by
cutting them off.

The richest
1,000 people in Britain
are twice as rich as they
were 10 years ago.

$1,000 invested
in the cocaine trade in 2014
would have been worth
$182,000 in 2015.

It would cost
£9 billion to buy one
of everything for sale
on Amazon.com.

After Christmas,
Britons return
£207 million worth
of unwanted gifts.

On New Year's Eve,
birds in the Netherlands
fly much higher than normal
to avoid the fireworks.

Police officers patrolling
Istanbul on New Year's Eve
dress up as Santa
to blend in.

Translated into English,
the five most common
Turkish surnames are
Brave, Rock, Iron,
Falcon and Steel.

In 2012,
no babies born in the UK were
named Cecil, Willie, Bertha, Fanny,
Gertrude, Gladys, Marjorie
or Muriel.

Babies can
recognise and make
all 150 sounds of the
world's 6,500 languages until
they are nine months old.

Lithuania has an annual
crawling race for babies.

Babies
born in winter start
crawling five weeks earlier
than those born
in summer.

Boys born in winter
are more likely to be
left-handed.

Right-handed
marmosets
are braver than
left-handed marmosets.

Asthmatic otters
can be taught to use
inhalers.

Baby rats
are known as
'kittens'.

There is an equivalent
of Match.com for
zoo animals.

In 2014,
a panda called Ai Hin
pretended to be pregnant
to get her own room
and more buns.

If the northern giant mouse lemur
were scaled up to human size,
its testicles would be as
big as grapefruit.

The world's smallest lemur
and the world's smallest chameleon
live on the same island.

The word
'Nile' means 'river',
so River Nile means
'River River'.

Eas Fors
waterfall on the
Isle of Mull means
'Waterfall Waterfall'
waterfall.

Torpenhow
in Cumbria means
'Hillhillhill'.

The Atlas Mountains,
the Appalachians and the
Scottish Highlands were
once all part of the same
mountain range.

Compasses don't work
on the highest mountain
in Mauritania.

The highest point
of Canada was only
determined
in 1992.

In 1787,
the top of Mont Blanc
was removed and is now
in a museum in the
Netherlands.

When Edmund Hillary
got to the top of Everest
he celebrated by peeing.

The largest and most distant
body of water so far discovered
is 30 billion trillion miles away,
with 140 trillion times more
water than Earth.

The distance travelled by
your blood every day is equivalent
to half the Earth's circumference.

The volume of urine created
by the world's population in a year
is almost identical to the UK's
annual water usage.

In 2006,
the words 'cyclists dismount'
on a road sign near Cardiff were
mistranslated into Welsh as
'bladder inflammation upset'.

The time spent
waiting for a bus
feels shorter if you wait
in an area full
of trees.

The first
London bus routes
weren't numbered but
colour-coded.

In the 1840s,
London bus drivers had
straps attached to their arms
that you tugged when you
wanted to get off.

The Maori word
for London is
Ranana.

Texas is
Norwegian slang for
'crazy'.

The Norwegian version
of the Mr Men book *Mr Bump*
is called *Herr Dumpidump*.

Every year,
thousands of Norwegian children
are sent to fake refugee camps
so they can experience
what it's like.

Dr Seuss
wrote a film that was banned
because it predicted the
Manhattan Project.

In 1964, the US
set off nuclear bombs
under Mississippi.

Project Orion
was a plan to use
nuclear weapons to
power spacecraft.

It's theoretically safe
to swim in a pool used to
store spent nuclear fuel,
as long as you stay
near the surface.

America's
nuclear weapons
are still controlled
by floppy discs.

Space-time
is a billion billion billion
times stiffer than steel.

It would take
136 billion sheets of A4
to print out the Internet.

Smartphone users
touch their phone
2,617 times a day.

Computers
cannot generate
random numbers.

Manta rays
are the only fish that
can recognise themselves
in a mirror.

The bristlemouth fish
is the most common
vertebrate on
the planet.

The genitals of
the male priapiumfish
are under its
chin.

Starfish
can regrow a
whole new body from
a single arm.

An injured
moon jellyfish grows
new tissue to remain
symmetrical.

If a bald eagle
loses a feather on one wing,
it sheds the same feather on the other
to maintain balance.

Shuttlecocks used in
professional badminton are made
of feathers from the left wing of a goose.
Feathers from the right wing
make them spin the
wrong way.

It is illegal in the US
to pick up and keep
bird feathers.

Orthodox Jewish couples
abstain from sex on Christmas Eve.
Rabbis used to advise them to
pass the time tearing
toilet paper instead.

1 in 3 children
pretend to believe in Santa Claus
to keep their parents happy.

Christmas presents in Greece
aren't delivered by Father Christmas
but by Saint Basil.

Saint Philip Neri,
'The Humorous Saint',
once shaved off half his beard
and always wore a cushion
on his head.

In 1567,
the man with the
world's longest-ever beard
broke his neck and died
after tripping over it.

Jerome Bonaparte,
the last of Napoleon's descendants
in America, died after tripping
over his dog's lead.

Dog-owners who pretend
not to see their dog defecating are
employing what sociologists call
'strategic non-knowledge'.

Prince Rupert of the Rhine
trained his dog to urinate when
it heard the enemy's name.

Dogs and cats
are 25% more likely
to get injured or sick
during a full moon.

Charles Cruft
also founded a cat show,
but it didn't
catch on.

During the
Second World War,
it was illegal to feed
milk to cats.

Ninjas used the
dilation of a cat's pupils
to tell the time.

There is no word for 'time'
in any Aboriginal language.

The ability to emit light
has evolved independently
at least 50 times in the
animal kingdom.

Falling into a
black hole would
turn you into
a hologram.

A person
who was invisible
wouldn't be able to
see anything.

To cure blindness,
ancient Egyptians poured
mashed-up pig's eye into
the patient's ear.

The earliest known
treatment for deafness was
to fill the ears with a concoction
of olive oil, red lead, ant's eggs,
bat's wings and goat's urine.

The first prosthesis,
found on a 3,000-year-old
Egyptian mummy,
was a toe.

With their eyes shut,
most people can't tell
which of their toes
is being prodded.

Anomia
is the inability
to remember
names.

Nelson Mandela's
real first name was Rolihlahla,
which means 'trouble-maker'
in Xhosa.

Max Factor's
real name was
Maksymilian Faktorowicz.

Names of
16th-century lipsticks include
Ape's Laugh, Smoked Ox
and Dying Monkey.

The world's
longest treadmill
was built for
wolves.

Australian sheep
have been bred so large
that farmers can't
shear them.

The Big Sheep is
the top tourist attraction
in Devon.

Descartes believed that a
drum made of sheep skin would
stay quiet if struck at the same time
as a drum made of wolf skin because,
even in death, the sheep would
be afraid of the wolf.

The first dog
to play Lassie was
called Pal.

The first
English teacher in Japan
was called Ranald MacDonald.

The first
ice cream on a stick
was called the Jolly Boy Sucker.

The third
most popular
ice cream van jingle is
the *Match of the Day* theme.

Ice cream is
solid, liquid and gas
all at the same time.

The earliest known
ice cream recipe recommends
flavouring it with
whale faeces.

The earliest known
book of manners advises:
'Do not attack your enemy
while he is squatting
to defecate.'

The ink from
a lasered-off tattoo
is later excreted
by the wearer.

Gunmen in
the Wild West didn't wear
holsters on their thighs,
or call themselves
'gunslingers'.

Jeans were first worn by
Genoan fishermen because
they were easy to take off
if they fell overboard.

The ancient Romans
considered wearing trousers
the mark of a barbarian.

When the Romans
first arrived in Britain,
they found the British uncouth
because they had so many
tattoos.

The Maoris
arrived in New Zealand
in 1300.

New Zealand's
Ninety Mile Beach
is 55 miles long.

1 in 100 Kiwis
are allergic to
kiwis.

Only 15% of the
population of Qatar are
Qatari.

Fungi
are responsible for
more deaths than malaria
and tuberculosis
combined.

Tuberculosis
was brought to
North America
by seals.

There is an ethnic group
in central India in which
nobody ever suffers
from back pain.

A group of
giraffes is called
a tower.

The maximum height
for cabin crew in the first
tiny Ryanair planes was 5' 2" –
the same as the current minimum.

The first time aeroplanes
were used by British police was
in the search for Agatha Christie
when she went missing in 1926.

Sherlock Holmes cases not
written up by Watson include
'A Full Account of Ricoletti of the
Club Foot and his Abominable Wife'
and 'The Politician, the Lighthouse
and the Trained Cormorant'.

Jack London, Hugh Walpole
and P. G. Wodehouse were all
published by Mills & Boon.

John le Carré's father
once seduced a woman
on a night train by
claiming to be
John le Carré.

Evelyn Waugh's
first wife's name was Evelyn.
They were known as He-Evelyn
and She-Evelyn.

Hitler wrote a sequel to *Mein Kampf*
but never published it in case
it affected the sales of
the original.

Hitler's
sister-in-law Bridget
wrote a memoir called
My Brother-in-Law Adolf.

During the Second World War,
the Allies considered dropping glue
onto Nazi troops to make them
stick to the ground.

The Nazis
didn't call themselves Nazis
because *Nazi* is German slang
for 'country bumpkin'.

British sailors in
the Second World War
wore tattoos of pigs and roosters
to protect against drowning.

In the first two years
of the First World War,
a soldier who broke a leg
had an 80% chance
of dying.

901 British babies
born in the First World War
were christened Verdun,
71 were called Ypres
and there were
15 Sommes.

The town of Ypres in Belgium
has a cat festival to commemorate
their former sport of tossing
cats from the bell tower.

Until 1993,
the location of the
Post Office Tower was
a national secret.

Gustav Eiffel
didn't design the
Eiffel Tower.

Newton's Cradle
was invented by
French physicist
Edme Mariotte.

American inventor
Buckminster Fuller
slept for just two
hours a night.

Thomas Edison
and Henry Ford
went on road trips
together.

Leonardo da Vinci
designed chairs made of cake,
a giant whisk as tall as a giraffe,
and a horse-powered
nutcracker.

ⓘ

'Generator' was
a name Crimean politicians
asked people to call their sons
in 2015 to bring attention to
the country's power crisis.

'Ruperts'
were dummy parachutists
dropped as decoys
on D-Day.

In 2013,
37 British babies were named Loki,
after the Norse god
of mischief.

In 2013,
Gary was a less popular
baby name in the UK than
either Loki or Thor.

Bluetooth is
named after Harald Bluetooth,
the Viking king who united
Norway and Denmark.

The anti-spam industry
is worth more than
the spam industry.

Selfies
kill more people
than sharks.

Young British adults
rate an Internet connection
as more important
than daylight.

The first email
had to be printed out
to be read.

Emails in
the Vatican are called
inscriptio cursus electronici.

Hydrangea serratifolia
means 'with serrated leaves'.
It actually has smooth leaves but
the original sample had
been nibbled.

Lichen aromaticus
has no aroma but the
original specimen arrived in
a perfumed envelope.

In the 16th century,
you could buy perfumed
'sweet gloves' to offset the fact
that glove leather was softened
by being steeped
in dog poo.

Catherine de' Medici
used poisoned gloves
to kill her enemies.

The golden dart frog,
the world's most toxic amphibian,
can't produce poison if
born in captivity.

The toxic ribs of
Spanish ribbed newts
burst out of their sides
to stab predators.

A gram of
scorpion poison
costs £415.

Scorpions
can have 12 eyes.

Antimatter
costs £17 billion
per gram.

There are 568
billionaires
in China.

China used more cement
between 2011 and 2013 than
the US did in the entire
20th century.

In the 19th century,
people with 'cement delusion'
believed they were made of
cement.

Charles VII of France
thought he was made of glass
and wrapped himself in blankets
to prevent his buttocks
shattering.

The carbon dioxide in
a bottle of champagne would
fill six bottles if stored
at normal pressure.

Ⓠ

More Guinness
is drunk in Nigeria
than in Ireland.

10 million
glasses of Guinness
are sold every day.

The apostrophe after
the letter 'O' in Irish names was
added by the British, who thought it
needed a link to the rest of the name.
Many Irish speakers
refuse to use it.

The area round Dublin under
British rule was called the Pale,
hence the expression
'beyond the pale'.

A 'swearing consultant'
was hired for the BBC sitcom
The Thick of It.

In 2014, US naturalist Paul Rosalie
went on the TV show *Eaten Alive*
to be swallowed by an anaconda,
but bailed out the moment the
snake attached its jaws
to his helmet.

The BBC's
most popular export is
Keeping Up Appearances.

Nine of the top 10
highest-rated TV programmes
in Portuguese history were
football matches.

F. Scott Fitzgerald
invented the idea of
offensive and defensive teams
in American football.

One in every 900 men
from American Samoa play in
the National Football League.

The crowd at
Seattle Seahawks games is
so loud that the US Geological Survey
uses the vibrations to calibrate
its seismographs.

US cities with teams
that reach the Super Bowl
suffer an 18% increase
in deaths from flu.

No Creek, Kentucky,
acquired its name after a
surveyor was overheard saying,
'Why, that's no creek at all.'

Truth or Consequences, New Mexico,
changed its name from Hot Springs
to get the radio quiz show
Truth or Consequences
to record there.

Whorehouse Meadow in Oregon was
renamed Naughty Girl Meadow in the 1960s
but was changed back again by
public demand.

Yakutat, Alaska,
is six times the size of the
state of Rhode Island but only
has a population of 662.

Q

Yuma, Arizona, is
the sunniest place in the world:
on any given day there is a
90% chance of sunshine.

92% of pop songs
that mention the Sun
are in a major key.

The 1956 edition of
Encyclopaedia Britannica
described rock 'n' roll as
'insistent savagery'.

Names of
Japanese rock bands include
Seagull Screaming Kiss Her Kiss Her,
Mass of the Fermenting Dregs
and Abingdon Boys School.

A Japanese person
who moves to America
doubles their chances of
fatal heart disease.

Until the 20th century,
a hangover meant
'unfinished
business'.

Drinking
water hardly helps
hangovers at all.

Every time
Alfred Hitchcock
drank a cup of tea,
he smashed the teacup.

Hitchcock bought up
all the copies of the novel
Psycho so people wouldn't
find out the ending.

Harper Lee's friends
gave her a year's wages
for Christmas 1956 so she
could take time off to finish
To Kill a Mockingbird.

Terry Pratchett
had 10 honorary doctorates
and was an honorary Brownie.

After he was knighted,
Sir Terry Pratchett made
his own sword out of
meteorites.

Finnish students carry
a doctoral sword to their
graduation ceremony.

Every evening at 10 p.m.,
it's a tradition for Swedish
students to open their windows
and start screaming.

The 1912 Stockholm Olympics
was the last time the gold medals
were made from pure gold.

If Sweden plays Denmark,
it's abbreviated to SWE–DEN;
the remaining letters spell
DEN–MARK.

Though Denmark is
the world's least corrupt country,
12% of Danes know someone
who's taken a bribe.

In Copenhagen,
there are more bicycles
than people.

The Tricycle Union
was founded in 1882 to
distance tricyclists from bicyclists,
who were considered
disgraceful.

The first motorcycles
were built in the 1860s
and were powered
by steam.

When Evel Knievel
starred in the 1977 film
Viva Knievel! he used
a stunt double.

Evel Knievel
holds the world record
for most bones broken
in a lifetime
(433).

A Japanese motorcycle
that runs on animal dung
has a toilet-shaped seat.

In Japan,
nightingale droppings
are used as a
face cream.

In 2008,
Japan and Britain
(without mentioning the war)
officially celebrated 150 years
of friendly relations.

During the Second World War,
experts claimed to be able to
identify pigeons with a
German accent.

In 2013,
a kestrel was arrested in Turkey
on suspicion of spying
for Israel.

It takes between 60 and 80
intelligence agents to monitor
a single terrorist suspect
round the clock.

The UK and Iran are the
only countries in the world to
have unelected clerics sitting
in the legislature.

When James Keir Hardie,
Britain's first socialist MP,
arrived at Parliament in 1892,
a police officer thought he was
there to mend the roof.

Between 2010 and 2015,
British MPs drank 625,464
cans and bottles of Coke, and
ate 659,470 chocolate bars.

Sir Kenelm Digby,
inventor of the modern wine bottle,
was a pirate whose father had tried to
blow up the Houses of Parliament.

Drinking one glass of wine
makes you more attractive;
drinking a second undoes
all the good work.

People pour
9% more white wine
into a glass
than red.

You'd need to do 60 squats
to offset the weight gain
caused by a large glass
of red wine.

In 16th-century Italy,
'corked' wine was thought to
have been spoiled by
a witch's urine.

The Soviet
588th Night Bomber regiment
was an all-female squadron
known by the Germans
as the 'Night Witches'.

In 1946,
Sergei Pavlovich Korolev
became the chief designer of
the Soviet missile programme.
Six years earlier, he had been
in a Gulag expecting to die.

The original 'flying saucers',
reported in 1947, were shaped
like boomerangs.

UFOs in the
Large Hadron Collider are
'Unidentified Falling Objects'.

In April 2016,
the Large Hadron Collider
was shut down after a
weasel fell into it.

Walruses
suffer from
dandruff.

Porcupines
eat canoe paddles.

Balsa wood
is mothproof.

85 million years
before butterflies existed,
there was another insect that
looked and acted exactly
like a butterfly.

In the early 1700s,
Lady Eleanor Glanville was
declared insane because she liked
collecting butterflies.

Both Saturn
and Jupiter began
as collections
of pebbles.

Some archaeologists think
the erection of Stonehenge was
primarily a team-building exercise.

In 2015, a 10-year scientific study
concluded that punching glass
is dangerous.

In 2014, two scientific journals
accepted a nonsense paper from a
made-up university co-authored
by 'Maggie Simpson'.

A scientific paper looking into
the spells of Harry Potter concluded
they would need magic to work.

The more people
believe in witchcraft,
the less they tend to give
to charity.

Q

The Bank of England
only owns two
gold bars.

Malaysian athletes who
win an Olympic gold medal
are also awarded a
solid gold bar.

US coins
last 20 times as long
as dollar bills.

A one-tiyin coin
in Uzbekistan is worth
one three-thousandth
of 1p.

Ecstasy, cocaine and heroin
are all more expensive
than gold.

As a penniless
young actor in a tiny bedsit,
Nigel Hawthorne survived
mainly on sultanas.

Jimmy Stewart was
a brigadier general in
the US Air Force.

J. B. Priestley claimed
George Bernard Shaw disliked
the Grand Canyon because it was
more important than he was.

A peacock's tail
is 60% of its entire
weight.

Dunnocks copulate
100 times a day, for a
tenth of a second
at a time.

Harris hawks
stand on each other's shoulders
to get a better view.

Ravens get stoned
by rubbing chewed-up
ants on their
feathers.

Drugs are
smuggled into prison by
stuffing them into dead birds
and hitting them over the fence
with a tennis racket.

In China,
it is illegal to
post erotic banana
videos online.

Humans can be
aroused by touching
a robot's genitals.

30% of objects
left in hotel rooms
are sex toys.

The happiest couples
are those who have sex
once a week.

A 'nookie-bookie'
is a pimp or madam.

Star Trek almost failed
to get a commission because
the pilot was too erotic.

Former England rugby captain
Phil Vickery is a qualified
cattle inseminator.

There are tunnels under
New York that were once used
to transport cattle to
slaughterhouses.

South African cows
wear reflective earrings
at night to make them
visible to drivers.

In 2010,
a Bulgarian councillor was
sacked for milking virtual cows
on the gaming app FarmVille
during budget meetings.

In the 18th century,
people washed their faces
and polished their shoes
with asses' milk.

The world's heaviest
newborn baby weighed
22 lb 8 oz.

Newborn babies
have accents.

First-born children tend to be
taller, fatter, more allergy-prone,
more cautious and have a higher IQ
than their younger siblings.

Ukrainians
are 13 times more likely
to die of heart disease
than the Japanese.

In the 1966 World Cup,
the Brazilians drank so much coffee
they were worried they would
be banned for doping.

In the 2014 World Cup,
Ecuadorean Enner Valencia
was on the ground feigning injury
four seconds after kick-off.

Before penalty shoot-outs,
Argentinian goalkeeper Sergio Goycochea
would urinate on the pitch
for good luck.

To distinguish
the two sides at the first
US college football game in 1869,
the home team wore
turbans.

San Marino's
national football team
has only ever won
one match.

In 1947,
English footballers' salaries
were capped at £12 a week.

An 18th-century
tradesman or clerk
took a year to earn what
a prostitute could make
in a month.

More than a billion people
in the modern world live
on no more than
$1 a day.

One in a million people
have four kidneys, but
most of them don't
know they do.

The word
'anticipation'
once meant money paid
as an advance
on salary.

1 in 16 of the
words you encounter
every day is
'the'.

The word 'ushers'
contains five pronouns:
us, she, he, her and hers.

'Hurkle-durkle' is a Scottish word
meaning to lounge around when
you should be up and about.

The word 'wow'
was popular in Scotland
for 400 years before it caught on
in the rest of the English–
speaking world.

Transposing 'a' for 'z',
'b' for 'y' and so on
in the word 'wizard'
produces 'draziw'.

At the 2011
World Scrabble Championship,
one player demanded another be
strip-searched after a letter
'G' went missing.

Q

Scrabble's inventor
assigned values to letters
by counting their frequencies
in the *New York Times*.

The word 'era' is a solution in
the *New York Times* crossword
about 20 times a year.

The New York City
Police Department
has 1.2 million open
arrest warrants.

Pinball is illegal
in Beacon, New York.

Q

New York
was originally called
New Angoulême.

'Manhattan'
is from the Algonquian
manahachtanienk, meaning
'the place we all got drunk'.

20% of
licensed attorneys
in the US have a
drinking problem.

Ancient Egyptians
had slaves who cooled
their wine with fans.

The first domestic fridge
was invented by a monk to
chill the monastery wine.

Einstein
patented a fridge.

Yoda
was based on
Einstein.

When Einstein solved
the problem of Mercury's orbit,
he had heart palpitations
and couldn't work
for three days.

Neptune was discovered
within an hour of astronomers
starting to look for it.

Saturn's moons
have volcanoes that
erupt ice.

In the last 20 years,
amateur stargazers have
discovered more comets than
all the astronomers in
history combined.

Anyone
can submit a name
for a new planet.

In the 19th century,
there were multiple sightings of
a non-existent planet
called Vulcan.

NASA's
Vehicle Assembly Building
is so big it has its
own weather.

Apollo 13 nearly
crashed on take-off but
a second malfunction fixed
the first malfunction.

Because its terrain is
so similar to the Moon,
Apollo astronauts trained
in Iceland.

Beer was illegal in Iceland
until 1989.

In 1783,
the eruption of
an Icelandic volcano
caused a deadly fog in
Britain that killed
20,000 people.

In 1874,
plans were drawn up
to take corpses from all over
Europe and cremate them
in Vesuvius.

A taxidermist
in Inverness-shire
makes sporrans from
roadkill.

121 bell-ringers
were killed by lightning in
Germany between 1750 and 1783,
due to a belief that church bells
drove away storms.

The 7th time
park ranger Roy Sullivan
was struck by lightning
happened shortly after
the 22nd time he'd
had to fight off
a bear with
his stick.

Florida has
more bear-hunters than bears.

More people are killed by
teddy bears than by grizzly bears.

A 'bugbear'
was a hobgoblin
in the shape of a bear.

You can
be allergic
to your own sweat.

The man who
discovered why we sweat
did so by getting into a sauna
with a dog, a steak
and an egg.

The man who
discovered the source of the Nile
accidentally shot himself with a rifle
while climbing over a stile.

The first westerner
to attempt to find Timbuktu died
after trying to cure an attack
of vomiting by drinking
sulphuric acid.

Families in Timbuktu
descended from the Moors
expelled from Granada in 1492
still have the keys to
their former homes.

The name Timbuktu
comes from a word meaning
'woman with a sticking-out
belly button'.

Mexico Tenochtitlan,
the name of the Aztecs' capital,
means 'Navel of the Universe'.

There is a
species of leech
that lives in the rectums
of hippopotamuses.

Hippopotomonstrosesquipedaliophobia
is an invented word meaning
'the fear of long words'.

The longest word in Bulgarian
means 'do not perform actions
against the constitution'.

'Semantic satiation'
is repeating a word so often
it sounds like nonsense.

The word 'bride' is
from an ancient root meaning
'to brew or make broth'.

A wedding of
100 guests at 10 tables
has 65 trillion trillion trillion
trillion trillion trillion trillion
seating possibilities.

From 1489 to 1493,
Leonardo da Vinci was a
wedding planner.

When women ovulate,
their faces get slightly redder,
but most men don't notice.

The thinnest skin
on the human body is
on the eyelids.

Fish-scaled geckos
escape predators by
literally jumping
out of their skins.

The Palmato gecko
drinks water off
its own eyeballs.

Sharks don't drink at all;
they absorb seawater
through their gills.

Female sharks
can store sperm in their bodies
for four years before using it.

The smallest shark
is less than 10 inches long
and glows in the dark.

Cockroaches
can see in the dark.

Frogs can
make their skin darker to
match their surroundings, but
it takes about two hours.

Murderous frogs featured
on Victorian Christmas cards,
along with children being
boiled in teapots and
mice riding
lobsters.

Mexico has a festival
where Nativity scenes
are carved out of radishes;
in 2014, they used 12 tons of them.

In 1494, Piero de' Medici
commissioned Michelangelo
to sculpt him a snowman.

The fake snow in
The Wizard of Oz and
White Christmas was
made of asbestos.

London City Airport confiscates
150 souvenir snow globes from
passengers every year.

Wonderpedia magazine was
pulled from airport shops after it ran
an article on how to build weapons
from things available in airports.

Flights from
JFK Airport in New York are
sometimes delayed so that
turtles can be moved
off the runways.

Vancouver Airport
has a bathroom
for dogs.

Vanuatu's
national anthem is
'Yumi! Yumi! Yumi!'

Algeria's national anthem
includes the line 'Oh France,
the day of reckoning
is at hand.'

Western Sahara's national anthem
urges its people to 'cut off
the head of the invader'.

From 1919 to 1948,
Korea's national anthem
was sung to the tune of
'Auld Lang Syne'.

Japanese department stores
play 'Auld Lang Syne'
to tell shoppers it's
closing time.

It is illegal in Japan
to make a human pyramid
more than five tiers high.

By the end of
the 19th century,
most Samurai had
desk jobs.

46% of Japan's population hide
when someone rings
the doorbell.

A gram of silver
can be extruded into a wire
over a mile long.

The weight of
Greenland's ice sheet
has made the country
bowl-shaped.

Nitrogen tri-iodide
is so volatile that it will
explode if a mosquito
lands on it.

An 'Insect of the Month' calendar
wouldn't have to repeat a species
for more than 80,000 years.

British wasps
eat 14 million kilos of
British insects
every year.

When it gets hot,
bees squirt water
at each other.

The bombardier beetle
defends itself by shooting a
noxious mixture of boiling chemicals
out of its bottom.

Only 10%
of dung beetles
roll dung.

The world's first
flying subterranean insect was
discovered in Croatia
in 2016.

The world's first
robot pizza-delivery service
opened in Brisbane
in 2016.

The first use of the
word 'snowmageddon' was in a
press release that went on to
apologise for
using it.

The world's first
tornado forecast took
place in 1948.

US weather forecasters
were forbidden to mention
tornadoes between
1887 and 1950.

The World Health Organization's
guidelines for avoiding Middle East
Respiratory Syndrome (MERS)
include not drinking
camel urine.

The froth
from a camel's mouth
was once used as a
contraceptive.

Ancient Egyptians
used onion juice as a
contraceptive.

In ancient Japan,
condoms were made
from tortoise shells
or animal horns.

In Venezuela,
condoms cost more
than $20 each.

Google searches for
'How to put on a condom'
peak at 10.28 p.m.

Retired Google engineer
Chade-Meng Tan had the
official job title 'Jolly Good Fellow
(Which nobody can deny)'.

Lord Byron's nickname
for William Wordsworth
was William Turdsworth.

In the First World War,
nicknames for tanks included
land creepers, whippets,
wibble-wobbles
and willies.

The first tank
ever built was called
Little Willie.

Tanks are
exempt from London's
congestion charge.

NASCAR driver Dick Trickle
drilled a hole in his helmet
so he could smoke
while driving.

750,000 tons
of cigarette butts
are dropped on the ground
around the world
each year.

Mount Etna
sometimes blows
smoke rings.

The 'Door to Hell'
is a crater in Turkmenistan
which has been burning
for more than 40 years.

Colonel Sanders's
first restaurant was in
Hell's Half Acre, Kentucky.

The 'Badlands' of
the Queensland outback
is the second-hottest place
on the planet.

Australians take
four days off work
each year due to
heat stress.

There's an
Australian wasp
with the scientific name
Aha ha.

Towns
in Australia are
plagued by a tumbleweed
called Hairy Panic.

The town
of Spa in Belgium
is where the word
'spa' comes from.

In the 12th century,
Kaifeng, the capital of China, was
home to a million people.

The Great Wall of China
was held together with
sticky rice.

Chinese children
are three inches taller
than they were
40 years ago.

Babies in Laos
are fed rice that has been
pre-chewed by their mothers.
It's called 'kiss-feeding'.

Baby bats
babble before they learn
to communicate
properly.

Female vampire bats
regurgitate blood to feed
hungry neighbours.

Watching horror films
makes your blood
thicken.

In the movie *Predator*,
the monster's blood was made from
the inside of a glow-stick
mixed with KY Jelly.

The film *Poltergeist*
used real human skeletons as props,
because they were cheaper
than plastic ones.

'Morgue hotels' in Japan
store bodies in their own
air-conditioned rooms until
a space at a crematorium
becomes available.

In 2016,
protestors in South Korea
created a march made entirely
of holograms.

In 1831,
protestors in Merthyr Tydfil
first raised the red flag as
a symbol of resistance.

In 1511,
protestors in Brussels
demonstrated against the government
by filling the city with dozens of
pornographic snowmen.

Men who
watch a lot of porn
have smaller-than-average
brains.

Ancient Egyptian mummies
were given fake penises
so they could have
sex after death.

In 2015, a rare Greek papyrus
containing the Gospel of John
was discovered on eBay.

At the Lost Property Office
in ancient Jerusalem, people shouted
about the thing they'd lost,
in the hope somebody
else might have
found it.

Kent Police
no longer accept lost property;
instead they direct enquiries
to Twitter or Facebook.

Over 50% of people on Facebook
use 'haha' if something's funny;
only 1.9% use 'lol'.

The most common time for people
to misspell 'Facebook' as 'Facbook'
is 3:08 a.m.

In 2008,
Chile issued 1.5 million
50-peso coins from 'Chiie'.
It was a year before
anyone noticed.

In 1992,
the president of Sri Lanka
changed the country's name to
Shri Lanka for good luck.
He was assassinated
the following year.

The remote Russian island Яя (Ya Ya) was
discovered in 2013 by a cargo helicopter.
The crew shouted 'Я, я!' – 'Me, me!'
('I saw it first, I saw it first!') –
and the name stuck.

The westernmost point
of the island of Misima in
Papua New Guinea is called
'Cape Ebola'.

The only inhabitants of
Big Major Cay island,
the Bahamas, are
feral pigs.

During the mating season,
crabs on Christmas Island
outnumber humans
by 20,000 to 1.

Boxing Day
in Scotland
used to be called
'Sweetie Scone Day'.

Red velvet cake was
invented by a food-colouring
manufacturer to sell
red food dye.

Shoppers are more likely
to buy a banana if it matches
the Pantone colour 12-0752
known as 'Buttercup'.

Insect droppings
are turning the
Taj Mahal
green.

Homer describes
honey as being green,
sheep as being violet
and Hector's hair
as dark blue.

Pugs were
the official dogs of
the House of Orange.

Short-legged dogs were
bred so that owners on foot
could keep up with them
on hunts.

Dogfish are
called dogfish because
they like to hunt in packs.

Ernest Shackleton had dogs called
Slobbers, Saint, Satan, Painful, Swanker,
Fluffy, Bummer and Bob.

When Shackleton's Antarctic expedition
got stuck in the ice in 1915, they had to
use the *Encyclopaedia Britannica* as
toilet paper, but the ship's doctor
saved the entry on scurvy.

Woody Harrelson's
father was a door-to-door
Encyclopaedia Britannica salesman
before becoming a contract killer.

Scurryfunge
is the hurried tidying of a house
after seeing someone about
to arrive at your door.

Neidbau
is German for a
building constructed for the
sole purpose of annoying a neighbour.

Alexander Fleming's neighbours
foiled a burglary at his house
and were rewarded
with some of his
special mould.

A *smellfungus*
is someone who always
manages to find fault.

Deodorant makes
men smell more manly,
but it doesn't work for men
who are already manly.

Ants can smell
the difference between
friends and foes.

Dolphins
can't smell
anything at all.

The four-eyed fish
has split pupils so it can
see above and below the water
at the same time.

African tigerfish
are the only fish known
to leap out of the water
and pluck birds
out of the air.

Parrotfish
coat themselves in
protective mucous pyjamas
at night and eat them for
breakfast each morning.

In the 18th and 19th century,
nightgowns were worn
in the daytime.

In mid-20th-century America,
a negligee was a shroud
for a corpse.

Nobody knows
why we sleep.

Eosophobia
is a dread of the dawn.

Uhtceare
is an Old English word
for lying awake before dawn
and worrying.

Rammist
is being irritable after
waking up too early.

Your brain is
at its biggest in the morning
and gradually shrinks as
the day goes on.

An embryo
has 200 billion
neurons in its brain,
but loses half of them
before it is born.

French queens
gave birth in public to prove
the baby was theirs.

Women at the court of Louis XVI
drew blue veins on their necks
and shoulders to emphasise
their noble birth.

In 1764,
the Palace of Versailles was
described as a cesspool of dead cats,
urine, excrement, slaughtered pigs,
standing water and mosquitoes.

The world's most
expensive toilet paper is
£825,000 a roll; it's hand-delivered
with a bottle of champagne.

When the New York Jets
played at Wembley in 2015,
they brought their own toilet paper
as they thought the British stuff
was too thin.

Dogs relieving themselves
on streetlights can corrode them
to the point of collapse.

People who
desperately need a pee
tell more convincing lies.

In 1630,
1 in 7 people in Bologna
were nuns.

There is a
holy theme park
in Buenos Aires where
nuns get in free.

In the 1960s and '70s,
nuns' urine was used by
pharmaceutical companies
to make fertility drugs.

Sticklebacks
lose the ability to urinate
when building their nests.

Fishing snakes
don't fish and
no one knows
how they got
the name.

One of the founding members
of the New York Stock Exchange
was a man called
Preserved Fish.

In March 2003,
the Ocean Journey aquarium
in Denver, Colorado, was bought
by a seafood restaurant.

Whales mourn
their dead.

Shakespeare's skull
is missing from
his grave.

Over the last 10 years,
the market for burial plots
has outperformed the overall
UK property market
by three to one.

The death adder
was originally the deaf adder
because it never ran away
from humans.

In China,
it is bad luck to give clocks
as presents because in Chinese
'giving a clock' sounds like
'going to a funeral'.

The first US alarm clock,
patented in 1787,
only rang at
4 a.m.

Broccoli
used to be known as the
'five green fingers of Jupiter'.

In 1862,
Prince William of Denmark
became king of Greece
after a referendum
in which he got
six votes.

A lobster
can squirt urine
seven times the length
of its body.

In 1325, Bologna
went to war with Modena
over a stolen bucket.

In 1943, the crew of a Halifax bomber
downed in the Atlantic survived
11 days in a dinghy by catching
fish with their underpants.

In 2011, a man was stopped
at Los Angeles Airport after his
four checked-in bags were found
to be full of water containing
240 live fish.

In 2005, there were plans
to make a 50-foot-tall robot of
Michael Jackson that would
roam the Nevada desert.

Michael Jackson
regularly made prank calls
to Russell Crowe.

Ravens will
dig up and rebury food
if they were seen hiding it by
a bird they consider
untrustworthy.

Woodpeckers have a third eyelid
which stops their eyes popping out
when drilling into wood.

In the 1890s,
Eugene Schieffelin set out to
introduce every bird mentioned by
Shakespeare into North America.
The US is now overrun by
200 million starlings.

Bearded tits
don't have beards
and aren't tits.

On 1 July 1937,
a Mrs Beard became
the first person to dial 999.

Early 999 calls
set off a klaxon and a flashing red light
to make sure operators knew
an emergency call
was coming in.

The oldest
surviving telephone directory is
from New Haven, Connecticut, in 1878.
It listed the names of all the
people with phones but
not their numbers.

A quarter of worker ants
never actually do
any work.

When food is scarce,
baby pea aphids climb
onto their mother's back
and suck her blood.

The beaded lacewing
stuns its prey by
farting on it.

The sea squirt
is the only animal that
eats its own brain.

Messages travel
through the brain
faster than an F1
racing car.

The space shuttle did
0–100 mph in 8 seconds,
the same as a 1968
Ford GT.

On 9 October 2013,
NASA's *Juno* spacecraft travelled
round the Earth at 50 times
the speed of a bullet.

The bullet
was invented thousands of years
before the gun.

In 17th-century Vermont,
it was illegal to go to church
without a gun.

Killington,
Smuggler's Notch,
Suicide Six and Mad River Glen
are ski resorts in Vermont.

Scots has
421 words
for snow.

The ground
beneath the Antarctic ice
is hotter than under 99% of
the rest of the planet.

Anders Celsius's scale
originally had the freezing
point of water at 100 degrees
and the boiling point at zero.

The boiling point of lithium
in degrees Celsius is
1,342.

In 2015,
Professor Colin Raston
won an Ig Nobel prize for
unboiling an egg.

In the 18th century,
chickens were known as 'cacklers'
and eggs were 'cackling farts'.

Until the 20th century,
'yolk' was often written
(and pronounced) 'yelk'.

The original
Humpty Dumpty
was a drink made by
boiling ale with
brandy.

The earliest woodcut of
Jack and Jill showed
two boys called
Jack and Gill.

Only female hops
are used to
make beer.

Male crucifix toads
glue themselves to females
during sex.

Yellow mealworms
eat Styrofoam.

Chewing
can help stop
earworms.

Bubblegum was
once prescribed as a
remedy for polio.

The placebo effect
accounts for up to 60%
of a painkiller's
effectiveness.

100 Americans
die each year by choking
on pen lids.

The lives of
Cher, Elizabeth Taylor and
Ronald Reagan were all saved by
the Heimlich manoeuvre.

When Reagan
became president in 1981,
he had all the solar panels removed
from the White House.

'D'oh!'
is defined by the
Oxford English Dictionary as
'expressing frustration at the
realisation that things have
turned out badly or
not as planned'.

In France,
Homer Simpson says '*T'oh*';
in Spain, he says '*Ouch!*'

A 'natural'
used to mean
an 'idiot'.

'A rumbling stomach'
is actually a rumbling of
the small intestine.

The phrase
'No Man's Land'
was first used in the
Domesday Book.

The land
that once connected
Great Britain to continental Europe
was called Doggerland.

Never Never Land
was an old name for
the sparsely populated
parts of Australia.

Narnia
(now called Narni)
is a real place in Italy.
C. S. Lewis saw the name
on an old Roman map.

After their first meeting,
C. S. Lewis wrote of J. R. R. Tolkien:
'No harm in him, only needs
a smack or so.'

In 1931,
both Hitler and Churchill
were hit by cars.

US boxer Daniel Caruso
was psyching himself up for a match
by punching himself in the face when
he broke his own nose and was
ruled unfit to compete.

Backpfeifengesicht
is German for a 'face
that needs hitting'.

Sneezes
can travel up to
200 feet.

Snakes
hear with their
jawbones.

A balloon's pop
is caused by the rubber
shrinking faster than
the speed of sound.

The equipment for the 2016
Rolling Stones concert in Havana
filled 61 sea containers
and a Boeing 747.

Ⓠ

Hummingbirds
'sing' with their
tail feathers.

Cauliflowers
grow so fast
you can hear them
doing it.

Cicadas
can 'switch off' their ears
to avoid being deafened
by their own singing.

New Forest cicadas are inaudible
to humans, so nobody knows
if there are any left
in the UK.

The only wild beavers
in the UK live on
the River Otter.

Napoleon had
50 identical
beaver-skin hats.

Genghis Khan's
earliest known ancestor
was a woman called
Alan the Fair.

Nell Gwyn's
name for Charles II was
Charles III because she'd
already had two lovers
called Charles.

Charles Dickens
helped stop P. T. Barnum
from moving Shakespeare's house,
brick by brick, to New York.

Charlotte Brontë's
school report said she
'writes indifferently' and
'knows nothing of grammar,
geography, history or
accomplishments'.

In the seven years
Wordsworth was Poet Laureate,
he didn't write a single
line of poetry.

Pope John Paul II
drew his own
comic books.

Retired characters
from the *Beano* include
Little Dead-Eye Dick, Cocky Dick,
Sticky Willie, Wandering Willie,
and Polly Wolly Doodle and
her Great Big Poodle.

The illustrator of the
first-ever nursery-rhyme book was
later sued for selling porn.

In 2016, 'porn' was
briefly overtaken by 'Brexit'
as the most searched-for
term on the Internet.

In the 1960s,
Internet was the
brand name for a
transistor radio.

Pope Francis
has never used the Internet
and hasn't watched TV
since 1990.

Pope Innocent VIII
was nicknamed 'The Honest' because
he was the first pope to admit
he had illegitimate children.

Pope John II was
the first pope to change his name.
He was originally called Mercurius
after the pagan god Mercury.

Mercury is
shrinking.

Russian rocket boosters are
blessed by an Orthodox priest
before they are ignited.

The Russians
have landed 10 times
as many probes on Venus
as NASA.

Earth
has eight times
as many trees as scientists
previously thought.

Four times as many
Lebanese live outside Lebanon
as inside it.

There are more
native Spanish speakers
in the US than
in Spain.

The oldest known
dialect of Spanish is
spoken in the US state
of New Mexico.

Caliche is
Latin American Spanish for
a crust of whitewash that
flakes off a wall.

41% of Americans
support the idea of
building a wall along the
Canadian border.

38% of the US
is north of the southernmost
point of Canada.

Canada
only gained independence
from Britain
in 1982.

The 1976 Montreal Olympics
is the only one in history
where the host country
failed to win a single
gold medal.

The coldest temperature
ever recorded in Canada is −63°C,
the same as the average
temperature
on Mars.

In 2015,
cold homes caused the
deaths of 9,000
Britons.

The blood of the
Antarctic notothenioid fish
contains antifreeze.

The film *Frozen*
took 3 million hours
to complete.

Frozen food was
invented by Clarence Birdseye,
after watching the Inuit in Canada
catch and freeze fish.

The actor who plays
Captain Birdseye
suffers from
seasickness.

Iggy Pop
has a cockatoo called
Biggy Pop.

Baron Rothschild
tried to impress Napoleon III by
by disguising his parrots as pheasants.
When shot, they would cry,
'Vive l'empereur!'

The Greeks painted eyes
on the bottom of glasses to
make it look like the drinker
was wearing a mask.

There are more mask shops
in Venice than butchers
or greengrocers.

Butchers in ancient Egypt
wore high heels to keep
blood off their feet.

1 in 5 women
cut the labels off their clothes
to hide the size.

The owner of Zara
is one of the two richest
people in the world.

A set of four car tyres,
encrusted with gold and diamonds,
broke the world record when
they were sold in 2016
for $600,000.

The man who
set the record time for
swimming the Panama Canal in 1959
was declared an honorary ship.

The ancient Egyptians built
the first Suez Canal in
the 6th century BC.

Canals have
plugs.

Baby sharks
are called
pups.

Captain Scott's
Antarctic expedition team hated
the taste of seal, so they overcooked it,
inadvertently destroying
all its vitamin C.

Shackleton's
Antarctic expedition found a
stowaway onboard who was allowed to stay
on condition he'd be the first to be
eaten in an emergency.

Some germs thrive
on soap dispensers because
they like to eat soap.

The first ATM
was based on a chocolate-bar
dispenser.

People who
regularly eat chocolate
are slightly thinner than
those who don't.

Obese people
see objects as 10%
further away than those
of average weight.

Lesbians
earn more than
straight women.

Only seven women in the world
may wear white to
meet the Pope.

The Colosseum
has banned people dressed
as Roman centurions.

The names
Linda, Alice, Lauren
and Elaine are banned
in Saudi Arabia.

It is illegal for
a wife to take her
husband's name in Quebec,
but obligatory
in Japan.

In 12th-century Ireland,
same-sex marriages were
performed in church.

Do You Trust Your Wife?
was a 1950s US TV game show
sponsored by a tobacco company.
It made one contestant change her
star sign from Cancer to Aries.

Camel cigarettes sponsored a 1940s TV
news show called *The Camel News Caravan.*
No one was allowed to be shown
smoking a cigar except
Winston Churchill.

Churchill looks grumpy
on the £5 note because the
photographer who took the picture
had just removed his cigar.

More British teenagers
smoke e-cigarettes than
ordinary cigarettes.

31% of
American teenagers
think they'll be famous
one day.

Three of the
top 10 Amazon best-sellers
in the US in 2015 were
colouring books
for adults.

Harvard
has a library of
rare colours.

There's a
bookshop in Tokyo
that only stocks one book
at a time.

Books containing
the word 'wine' and the
names of foreign pets
are banned in Iran.

'Stereotype' and 'cliché'
were both originally
printing terms.

The tune to
'Hark the Herald Angels Sing'
was written by Mendelssohn to
commemorate the invention
of the printing press.

⊕

The tune of
'God Save the Queen' was once
the best-known tune in the world
and the national anthem
for 20 countries.

The BBC's
first outside broadcast
was a duet between a cellist
and a nightingale.

Nightingales
frequently break
EU health and safety regulations
on noise pollution.

In 2016,
the Swiss city of Lausanne
banned silent discos for
being too noisy.

In 1936,
Leicester was the
second-richest city
in Europe.

According to
anthropologist Kate Fox,
England's national catchphrase
is 'Typical!'

Obsolete English words dropped by
the *Oxford English Dictionary* include
'growlery' (a room to growl in),
'brabble' (to quarrel) and
'cassette-player'.

Clatterfart,
blabberer, bablatrice and
nimble-chops all mean
'chatterbox'.

A 'gossip' was
originally a 'god-sibling'
or godparent.

The king of the Belgians
is automatically godfather to
all the seventh sons
in his country.

The Belgian city of Bruges
has an underground
beer pipeline.

The Rarámuri of Mexico
christen their babies
with beer.

Venezuela is
running out of beer.

Carlsberg
gave Niels Bohr
a house with free beer on tap
as a thank-you for winning
the Nobel Prize in physics.

In 1855, James Harrison,
a Scot living in Australia,
patented a beer cooler
that was the size
of a house.

Wilhelm Röntgen
refused to patent the
X-ray machine he'd invented
so that everyone could
benefit from it.

A new musical instrument was
invented and a new concert hall
built for the premiere of
Wagner's *Ring* cycle.

When rock 'n' roll music
was banned by the USSR in the 1950s,
Russians pressed bootleg copies
onto discarded X-rays and
called it 'bone music'.

The first full-length
porn movie filmed by drones
was called *Drone Boning*.

Mark Twain
invented and patented
the bra-strap clasp.

Microsoft was founded
closer in time to the invention
of the ballpoint pen
than to today.

Mike Rowe's
domain name
MikeRoweSoft.com
caused a legal dispute with
Microsoft.

The legal concept of negligence
was established in 1932, when
a woman found a snail
in her ginger beer.

The 18th-century dentist
Pierre Fauchard recommended
using urine as a
mouthwash.

The 18th-century painter
Johan Zoffany was shipwrecked
in the Andaman Islands
and ate a sailor.

Painting
a male barn owl's chest
a darker colour makes him
more desirable to females.

Great reed warblers
spend winter practising
their summer songs.

Racing pigeons
speed up when flying
through polluted air.

By eating and
excreting doves,
a single cougar can plant
94,000 seeds a year.

It's against the law
to bring potato seeds
into the UK.

There are over
700 British cheeses,
but most Britons can
only name four.

Shropshire Blue cheese
was invented in
Inverness.

You can buy
bonds backed by
Parmesan
cheese.

In the Second World War,
the Bank of England's canteen
was moved to the vault.

MasterCard's
New York headquarters are on
Purchase Street.

A 2015 study found
that banks give better deals
on loans immediately
after a robbery.

The most expensive transfer fee
in British women's football was for
a fifth of what Wayne Rooney
earns in a single week.

Manchester United has
spent more money on players in
the last three years than Leicester City
has in the 132 years since
it was founded.

The first
performance-enhancing drug
used in baseball was pulverised
guinea-pig testicles.

The owners
of Leicester City FC also
own the world champion
elephant polo team.

The king of Thailand
offered elephants as a gift
to President Lincoln,
but he declined.

JFK once wrote a letter
to his mother asking her not to
contact Nikita Khrushchev
without his permission.

Until the assassination of JFK,
it was not a federal crime to
to murder a US president.

In 1954,
President Eisenhower's motorcade
gave a lift to two hitch-hikers.

President Obama
is the only person outside HBO
allowed to watch advance screenings
of *Game of Thrones*.

At Queen Victoria's coronation
they accidentally missed out
a page of the ceremony and
had to call her back.

Queen Victoria's
first name was
Alexandrina.

Names of other
European monarchs
include Alfonso the Slobberer,
Albert with the Pigtail, and
Ivaylo the Cabbage.

Krill
smells like
boiled cabbage.

According to
the *British Medical Journal,*
farting on a Petri dish from 5 cm away
only results in bacterial growth
if the farter is naked.

Each person
is surrounded by
their own unique cloud
of bacteria.

Bacteria
invented the
wheel.

Cave paintings of
horses often have five legs;
when lit by fire, this creates
the illusion of movement.

Kubla Khan's niece agreed to
marry any man who beat her at
wrestling, but demanded payment
in horses if she were to win.
She died unmarried with
100,000 horses.

The deaths of two-thirds of
people in the world
go unrecorded.

According to
Isaac Newton,
the world will end
in 2060.

The last census
in Lebanon took place
in 1932.

The last words of
Franklin D. Roosevelt were:
'I have a terrific headache.'

When Henrik Ibsen's nurse
told him he was looking better,
he said, 'On the contrary,'
and died the next day.

According to psychics,
the best place in Britain to
contact the dead is
Eastbourne.

ⓘ

Art
is older than
humanity.

Since the first crew left for
the ISS on 31 October 2000,
there has not been a single day
when the entire human race
has been on Earth.

In the last 50 years,
insects' footsteps
have become
quieter.

The Lord of the Rings
ends in the year
1342.

Index

This is here to help you find your favourite bits.
Like the facts themselves, we've kept it as simple as we can.

[337]

of paradise 117; Clarence Birdseye 311; birth 283; birthdays 140, 152; births 103; black holes 196; bladders 186; Tony Blair 77; blessings 132, 308; blindness 196; Blockbuster Video 149; blood 186, 270, 271, 292, 311, 313; blowholes 85; blowing 47; blowtorches 11; Harald Bluetooth 211; Body Mass Index 176; Niels Bohr 324; Bolivia 100; Bologna 285, 289; Bolton 9; bombing 127; James Bond 56; Booker Prize 168; books 138, 320; bookshops 320; boom and bust 3; boomerangs 229; boredom 2, 136; Bosnia 78; botox 71; bottoms 253, 262; boulders 9; bowls 261; boxing 301; Boxing Day 276; braces 117; brain 67; brain cells 72; brains 72, 93, 272, 282, 292; brakes 125; branches 76; Marlon Brando 163; bras 148, 172, 325; Brazil 87, 118; bread 97, 144; breakfast 138, 281; breath 115; brewing 84; Brexit 306; bribery 55, 96, 224; bricks 26; brides 254; bridges 9, 10; briefcases 14; Brisbane 263; Britain 166, 169, 202, 226, 227, 284, 300, 304, 322, 328; broccoli 288; broken bones 20, 225, 301, 207; Charlotte Brontë 305; broth 254; brothers-in-law 206; brownies 222; Robert Browning 53; Bruges 323; Brussels 272; Bryony 124; buckets 289; Richard Buckminster Fuller 209; Buddhism 35, 111; Budweiser 83; Buenos Aires 285; Bugatti 73; buildings 248; Bulgaria 33, 238, 253; bullets 293; Battle of Bunker Hill 48; burglary 279; burials 287; Burundi 33; buses 187; George H. W. Bush 127, 142; butchers 313; butter 44; butterflies 231, 158; buttocks 215; buttons 37; Lord Byron 26

C-3PO 45; cabbage 333; cabin crew 205; Cadbury 166; cafeterias 111, 329; cakes 209; calendars 261; California 77, 85, 144, 165; California gulls 77; calories 174, 228; calves 128; Cambodia 96; camels 264; camouflage 42, 256; campanology 250; Canada 59, 85, 185, 309, 310, 311; canals

85, 280; Domesday Book 300; Donald 127; donkeys 121; door-to-door salesmen 278; doorbells 260; doors 146; doping 240, 330; double-cross 150; doves 328; dreadnought 32; dreaming 66; drinking 111, 116, 175, 221, 245, 255; driving 73, 96; drones 85, 325; drowning 207; drugs 236, 285, 330; drumming 38, 199; Dubai 54; Dublin 91, 216; ducklings 144; ducks 144; dummies 210; dung beetles 262; dunnocks 235; dye 276; Bob Dylan 119

e-cigarettes 319; eagles 192; earrings 238; ears 171,197, 303; Earth 153, 308, 336; earthquakes 218; earwax 59; earworms 297; Eastbourne 335; *EastEnders* 6; Clint Eastwood 127; eating 30, 36, 46, 81, 117, 147, 171, 173, 176, 270, 292, 297; eBay 273; ebola 275; economists 3; Ecstasy 234; Ecuador 240; Edinburgh 73; Thomas Edison 209; eggs 112, 295; Eiffel Tower 208; Albert Einstein 246; Dwight D. Eisenhower 331; elections 124; electricity 81; elephant polo 330; elephant shrews 47; elephants 47, 330, 331; Elizabethans 10; elms 75; email 212; embalming 44; embryos 283; emergencies 22, 291; emoji 135; emotions 135; *The Empire Strikes Back* 8; *Encyclopaedia Britannica* 220, 278; end of the world 334; enemies 194, 201, 213; energy 161, 210; energy drinks 39; English Channel 65; equator 118; error 404; escapes 55, 255; Ethiopia 156; etiquette 201; Etna 267; euphemisms 81; Europe 98, 300; euros 14; Everest 185; evolution 196; Ewoks 45; exciting 2; execution 95, 139; exhibitions 77; expense 45, 284, 314; extinction 164; eyeballs 41, 255; eyelids 255, 290; eyes 89, 197, 214, 280, 312

face cream 225, 238; Facebook 87, 273, 274; faces 68, 254; Max Factor 198; faeces 23, 92, 120, 158, 172, 194, 201, 213, 225, 262,

276, 283, 328; falling over 121, 194; *Fallout 4* 138; falsehoods 102, 183, 232, 240; fame 319; fan clubs 29; fancy dress 65; fanfares 78; fans 115, 245; farming 164; FarmVille 238; farting 17, 292, 295, 333; fashion 283; fat 157; fathers 206; fault 279; feathers 12, 192, 303; feet 121, 134, 147; festivals 257; fezzes 139; films 225; Find the Lady 72; fines 96; fingerprints 18; fingers 17, 288; Finland 33, 223; fire 54, 334; firefighters 54; fireworks 180; first-borns 239; First World War 109, 207; fish 31, 32, 85, 138, 158, 169, 174, 191, 280, 285, 286, 311; fish tanks 169; fishermen 202; fishing 286, 289; F. Scott Fitzgerald 218; flatworms 72; flavours 201; Flea 50; Fleet Street 60; Alexander Fleming 279; flesh 124; flies 27; floating 65; flocks 118; floppy discs 189; Florida 88, 140, 250; flowers 50, 95; flushing 23; 'Fly Me to the Moon' 152; flying 42, 59; flying saucers 229; Errol Flynn 163; fog 60, 157, 249; follicle mites 68; Henry Fonda 163; food colouring 276; football, 118, 217, 239, 240, 241, 330; footballers 119, 241, 330; footsteps 336; Ford Fiesta 146; Henry Ford 209; Foreign Secretary 69; forests 76; forgetting 103; George Formby 29; Formica 169; Formula One 293; formulae 43; fossils 4; Fox News 60; France 6, 70, 88, 125, 169, 259, 283; Benjamin Franklin 12, 13, 64, 141; fraud 120; French 62, 70, 88, 89, 162, 299; fridge-freezer 54; fridges 246; friends 38, 105, 226, 280; frisbees 107; frogs 46, 122, 213, 256; frowning 5; *Frozen* 311; frozen food 311; fruit flies 27; frustration 299; fuel 1, 16, 108; full 124; full moon 195; funerals 287; fungi 204; fur 6, 304

Clark Gable 107; Gaelic 110, 216; gambling 78; *Game of Thrones* 332; Greta Garbo 163; gardens 117; garlic 62; gas masks 172; gases 201; gates 9; geckos 46, 255; geese 10, 12; generators 210; genitals 113, 191, 236; Genoa 202; geologists

highwaymen 95; Edmund Hillary 185; hills 184; Hippocrates 19; hippopotamuses 253; Alfred Hitchcock 221; hitchhiking 331; Adolf Hitler 163, 206, 301; hitting 95; hobgoblins 251; holidays 62, 95; Hollywood 148; Sherlock Holmes 205; holograms 196, 272; Homer 277; honesty 307; hooting 105; hops 296; Horlicks 40; horns 265; horseradish 19; horses 58, 133, 134, 334; hotdogs 71, 145; hotels 104, 236, 271; Harry Houdini 163; House of Orange 277; houses 305; human pyramids 260; humanity 336; hummingbirds 303; humour 193; Humpty Dumpty 296; Hungary 105; hunting 250, 277; hydrangeas 212

Henrik Ibsen 335; ice 123, 247, 261, 278; ice cream 200, 201; ice cream vans 200; Iceland 248, 249; Icelandic 62; icicles 22; idioms 89; idiots 299; Ig Nobel Prizes 295; ignorance 63, 194, 197; illegitimate children 307; illness 133; imitation 26; immigration 203; independence 310; India 204; Indiana Jones 9; Indonesia 33; inflatables 25; influenza 133, 149, 218; ingredients 39; injuries 11, 207, 240; ink 201; insanity 231; insects 231, 261, 263, 276, 292, 336; instant messaging 87; International Space Station 21, 24, 115, 336; Internet 26, 57, 170, 190, 211, 306; intestines 299; Inuit 311; invasive species 106, 164, 269; Inverness 328; investigations 55; investment 179; invisibility 196; iPhone 161; Iran 47, 227, 320; Iraq 47; Ireland 90; Irish 216; Isle of Mull 184; Israel 226; Istanbul 180; Italian 88; Italy 88, 92, 228, 300; itches 110

Jack and Jill 296; jackass 121; Michael Jackson 289; Japan 38, 59, 69, 91, 126, 200, 220, 225, 226, 260, 265, 271, 317; jargon 120; jaws 302; jays 178; jeans 202; Thomas Jefferson 12; jellyfish 174, 192; Jerusalem 273; Jesus Christ 128; jet-packs

54; jets 73; jobs 265; Steve Jobs 37; jokes 53; journalists 60; joy 104; Judaism 193; jumping 280; junk 21; Jupiter 231, 288

kangaroo mice 165; kangaroo rats 165; kangaroos 65; Kansas 92; *Keeping Up Appearances* 217; John F. Kennedy 152, 331; Kent 273; Kentucky 219; Kenya 32; kestrels 226; kettles 6; keyboards 17, 88; keys 252; KFC 173, 268; Genghis Khan 304; Nikita Khrushchev 64, 331; kidneys 242; Captain James T. Kirk 8; kiss 46, 94, 270; kitchens 30; kittens 182; kiwi fruit 203; klaxons 291; Evel Knievel 225; Korea 259; Kosovo 32; krill 333; Kubla Khan 334; KY Jelly 271

labels 159; Labrador 84; lamas 44; Lancashire 145; landing 7; languages 45, 135, 181; Laos 270; Large Hadron Collider 16, 229; Las Vegas 167; lasagna 110; Lassie 200; last words 335; Latin 53, 123, 158, 212; laughing 89, 274; laurel 297; Lausanne 321; law 88, 140, 236, 294, 326; lawsuits 125; laxatives 44; laziness 292; John le Carré 206; lead 159; leaf-blowers 47; learning 47; leather 213; leaves 212; Lebanon 308; Christopher Lee 163; Harper Lee 17, 222; leeches 253; left 120; left-handedness 182, 192; Lego 25, 26; legs 42, 117, 277; Leicester 322; Leicester City 330; lemmings 23; lemurs 183; leprosy 52; lesbians 316; letters 137, 142, 143, 163, 331; lettuce 116; C. S. Lewis 300; Liberia 100; libraries 138; lichen 212; life 2; lifts 36, 131; light 196; lightning 250; lights 78, 108, 291; limpets 103; Abraham Lincoln 142, 331; lions 145; lips 110, 171; lipstick 198; liquids 201; literacy 34; lithium 295; Lithuania 181; littering 267; lizards 110; loans 329; lobster 288; Loch Ness Monster 29; locks 12; locusts 81; Loki 210; lol 274; London 61, 74, 75, 81, 95, 175, 187, 266; Jack London 205; Pippi Longstocking 137; *The Lord of the*

R2-D2 45; racehorses 134; races 181; Sergei Rachmaninoff 58; Radcliffe 145; radio 150, 219, 306; radishes 257; *Raiders of the Lost Ark* 9; railways 126, 141, 162; rain 41, 61, 62, 157, 160; rainforests 75; random numbers 190; randomness 35; rats 78, 182; ravens 235, 290; reading 36; Ronald Reagan 12, 142, 298; recognition 191; red 254; red flags 272; Red Hot Chili Peppers 50; red velvet cake 276; referendums 288; refugee camps 188; refunds 77; regeneration 191; regurgitation 270; reincarnation 140; relations 51; remoteness 114; repetition 102, 129, 150, 253; repetition 102, 129, 150, 253; research 43; restaurants 31, 81, 110, 176, 286; rewards 279; rheumatism 81; ribs 213; rice 269; rickets 5; rings 153; rivers 184, 304; road trips 209; roadkill 249; roads 96; roaring 4; robots 40, 85, 236, 263, 289; rock music 220; rock 'n' roll 154, 220, 325; rock stars 50; rockets 33, 116, 308; rocks 154; Gene Roddenberry 19; Rolling Stones 302; Romans 75; Rome 52; Wilhelm Röntgen 324; roofs 227; Wayne Rooney 330; Franklin D. Roosevelt 13, 335; Theodore Roosevelt 13; Baron Rothschild 312; Rotterdam 83; roulette 87; roundabout 20; Royal Mail 143; Royal Navy 49, 168; RSPB 177; rubber 302; rubber gloves 29; rugby 118, 237; rulers 127; rum 168; rumbling 299; Rupert 210; Prince Rupert of the Rhine 194; Russia 96, 97, 169, 275, 308; Russian Orthodox Church 308; Ryanair 205

sabre-toothed cats 5, 16; sacrifice 147; St Patrick's Day 71; saints 193; saliva 110, 148, 264, 332; Samurai 260; San Marino 241; Earl of Sandwich 81; sandwiches 81, 146; Santa Claus 180, 193; sarcasm 124; Satan 335; Saturn 231, 247; Saudi Arabia 155, 317; sauna 169, 251; sausages 70, 71; scared 173; schools 305; science 119; scientists 2, 119; scissors 19;

257, 294; snow globes 258; snowmageddon 263; snowmen 257, 272; soap 70, 315; sociology 176; sociopaths 164; socks 67, 123; Socrates 122; solar panels 298; soldiers 25, 109; solids 201; songs 152; sound 41, 303; sound effects 8, 9, 107; South Africa 238; South Korea 69, 272; South Sudan 147; Soviet Union 151, 152, 229; space 21, 22, 103, 116, 186, 247, 336; space shuttle 293; space-time 190; spacecraft 189; Spain 5, 309; spam 211; Spanish 299, 309; Spartans 124; spas 269; special effects 271; speed 79, 96, 293, 302, 303; speed of sound 302; Herbert Spencer 102; sperm 27, 82, 112, 256; sperm banks 82; sperm whales 172; Spider-Man 122; spiders 42; spies 163, 226; spirals 116; spoilers 222; *SpongeBob SquarePants* 113; sponges 173; sponsorship 318; spores 160; sporrans 249; sprouts 28; squats 228; squirrels 142, 177; Sri Lanka 274; stabbing 107; stamps 143; standardisation 156; standing 23; *Star Trek* 19, 237; *Star Wars* 8, 25, 45, 158; Starbucks 78; starfish 191; starlings 290; stars 1, 247; starvation 40, 46; state of emergency 101; static electricity 50; Statue of Liberty 130; statues 130; steam 224; Jimmy Stewart 234; stick insects 86; sticking 46; stiffness 190; stock exchange 286; Stockton-on-Tees 130; stomachs 299; Stonehenge 231; Stormtroopers 25; stowaways 315; strangers 52; strangling 20; straps 187; streakers 141; streetlights 284; stress 86; students 223; stunt doubles 225; stupidity 35; Styrofoam 297; submarines 169; sucking 175, 200; Suez Canal 130, 314; suffocation 85, 115; suits 102; sulphuric acid 252; sultanas 234; Sun 1, 114, 161; sunset 155; sunshine 220; suntans 1; supermarkets 78; suppositories 44; survival of the fittest 102; sushi 85; swearing 53, 217; sweat 251; Sweden 34, 35, 223; sweetness 276; sweets 136; swimming 64, 65, 189, 314; swimming pools 64; swords 11, 222; Sydney 80; symmetry 192

262, 295; water balloons 123; water pistols 99; waterfalls 184; Battle of Waterloo 48; Evelyn Waugh 206; WD40 176; wealth 179, 322; weapons 258; weasels 230; weather 248; weather forecasts 61, 263; weddings 16, 254; weeks 155; weighing 178; weight 1, 8, 239; Wellington boots 123; H. G. Wells 163; Wembley Stadium 51; John Wesley 97; Western Sahara 259; Wetherspoons 77; whales 85, 159, 171, 286; WhatsApp 87; wheels 333; whisks 209; whisky 110, 116; whistling 105; white 114, 317; *White Christmas* 257; White House 13, 298; whitewash 309; Walt Whitman 141; WHO 264; Wi-Fi 108, 130; wigs 10; Wikipedia 26; Wild West 202; Prince William of Denmark 288; William the Conqueror 111; willies 101, 181, 266, 306; WIMPs 102; wind 76; Windhoek 175; windows 13; Windows XP 169; Windsor 80; wine 97, 228, 245, 320; wine bottles 227; winter 181; wires 261; witchcraft 232; witches 228; *The Wizard of Oz* 257; wizards 243; P. G. Wodehouse 205; Wolverine 8; wolves 199; women 53, 54, 67, 79, 296, 317; wonder 103; *Wonderpedia* magazine 258; wood 4; woodpeckers 290; words 135, 149, 157, 242, 253, 322; William Wordsworth 266, 305; work 41; working 292; World Cup 240; world records 125, 138, 225, 314; worms 112; worry 10, 282; wow 243; wrens 58; Wright brothers 82; writing 136; wrongness 154, 159

X-Men 8; X-rays 324, 325; Xhosa 198

yachts 73; Yoda 246; yolks 296; Ypres 208

Zara 313; zombies 132; zoos 183